Editorial Project Manager
Lorin Klistoff, M.A.

Editor-in-Chief
Sharon Coan, M.S. Ed.

Illustrator
Sue Fullam

Cover Artist
Brenda DiAntonis

Art Manager
Kevin Barnes

Art Director
CJae Froshay

Imaging
Rosa C. See

Product Manager
Phil Garcia

Publisher
Mary D. Smith, M.S. Ed.

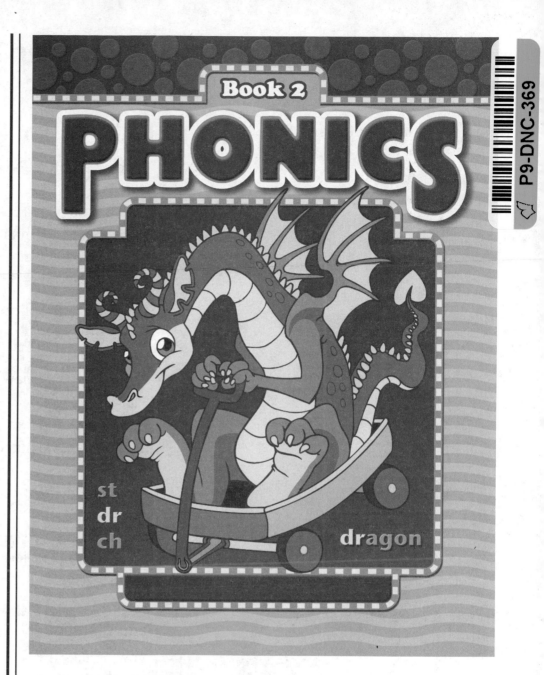

Book 2

PHONICS

st
dr
ch

dragon

Authors

Kathy Dickinson Crane & Kathleen Law

Teacher Created Resources, Inc.
6421 Industry Way
Westminster, CA 92683
www.teachercreated.com
ISBN: 978-0-7439-3016-1
©2004 Teacher Created Resources, Inc.
Reprinted, 2009
Made in U.S.A.

Table of Contents

Introduction

Systematic phonics instruction has been determined by research to be an important component of reading instruction. With phonics, students can make sound-symbol connections and begin to decode words.

Current research indicates that students need numerous opportunities to practice phonics skills. It must also be a part of reading instruction well beyond beginning reading. This workbook, *Phonics: Book 2*, provides practice in phonics skills for developing readers.

Phonics: Book 2 is part of a three-book series. As the second workbook in this companion series, *Phonics: Book 2* provides a practice and review of letters and sounds. Although alphabet recognition and phonemic awareness skills are reinforced, the emphasis is on phonics. A phonics rule is presented as the related skill is introduced. Students have multiple opportunities to apply each rule.

This workbook has been designed as a tool for additional practice for students developing more advanced reading skills. Consonants, vowels, blends, and digraphs are reviewed. Diphthongs, prefixes, synonyms, antonyms, and homonyms are introduced. Practice in all of these areas helps students move to a higher level on the reading continuum.

As students begin to read, it is important that skills and strategies be developed to ensure fluency and independence. The activities in this workbook present and review important reading skills and provide an opportunity for independent practice of these reading skills. When used in conjunction with a phonics-based reading program, this workbook will strengthen the learner's ability to read.

UNIT 1
Initial, Medial, and Final Consonants

Initial Consonants

Directions: Say the name for each picture below. Print both the capital and lowercase letters that represent its beginning sound.

Initial Consonants

Directions: Say the name for each picture below. Print the missing letter that represents its beginning sound. Trace the whole word.

1. _____ iger

2. _____ og

3. _____ at

4. _____ ear

5. _____ ouse

6. _____ ion

7. _____ itten

8. _____ oose

9. _____ ish

10. _____ orse

11. _____ ewt

12. _____ arrot

13. _____ at

14. _____ eal

15. _____ alrus

16. _____ -ray

Initial Consonants

Directions: Say the name for each picture below. Fill in the bubble beside the letter that makes the beginning sound in each word.

1. ○ k ○ t ○ b

2. ○ c ○ f ○ d

3. ○ f ○ j ○ r

4. ○ x ○ y ○ z

5. ○ d ○ b ○ p

6. ○ d ○ p ○ b

7. ○ m ○ n ○ b

8. ○ p ○ q ○ b

9. ○ c ○ s ○ b

10. ○ f ○ b ○ l

11. ○ q ○ p ○ b

12. ○ c ○ d ○ s

13. ○ f ○ t ○ l

14. ○ b ○ g ○ r

15. ○ v ○ z ○ w

16. ○ n ○ b ○ h

Initial Consonants

Directions: Change the beginning sound of the underlined word to complete each rhyme below. Print the word on the line and illustrate your sentence.

1. The <u>cat</u> was wearing a _____.

2. The <u>dog</u> sat on a _____.

3. The <u>pig</u> was dancing a _____.

4. The <u>sheep</u> was driving a _____.

5. The <u>goat</u> sailed on a _____.

6. The <u>mouse</u> lived in a _____.

7. The <u>fox</u> is in a _____.

8. The <u>king</u> wore a _____.

9. The <u>rock</u> landed on a _____.

10. The <u>duck</u> sat in a _____.

Initial Consonants

Directions: Change the letters that make the beginning sound to make new words. Write the new words on the lines.

1. Change | bread | to
2. Change | luck | to
3. Change | cat | to
4. Change | dog | to
5. Change | fuzz | to
6. Change | rag | to
7. Change | big | to
8. Change | tar | to

Final Consonants

Directions: Say the name for each picture below. Print the letter for its ending sound.

1.

2.

3.

4.

5.

6.

7.

8.

9.

10.

11.

12.

13.

14.

15.

16.

Final Consonants

Directions: Say the name for each picture below. Print the missing letter that represents its ending sound. Then trace the whole word.

1. spoo_	2. for_	3. cu_	4. bow_
5. be_	6. chai_	7. stoo_	8. ru_
9. ligh_	10. bo_	11. tu_	12. lea_
13. fil_	14. dres_	15. des_	16. bar_

Final Consonants

Directions: Say the name for each picture below. Fill in the bubble beside the letter that makes the ending sound in each word.

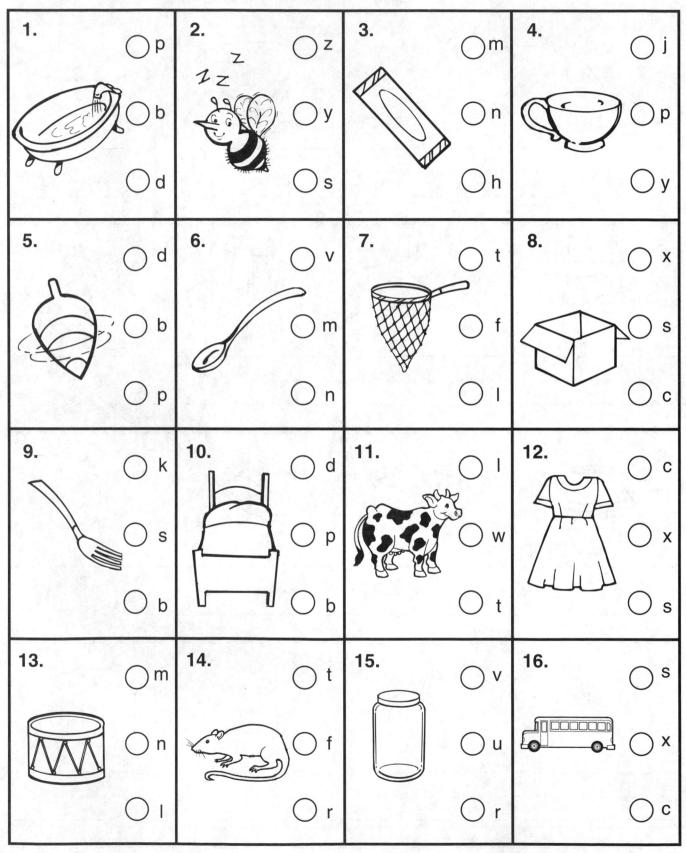

1.
○ p
○ b
○ d

2.
○ z
○ y
○ s

3.
○ m
○ n
○ h

4.
○ j
○ p
○ y

5.
○ d
○ b
○ p

6.
○ v
○ m
○ n

7.
○ t
○ f
○ l

8.
○ x
○ s
○ c

9.
○ k
○ s
○ b

10.
○ d
○ p
○ b

11.
○ l
○ w
○ t

12.
○ c
○ x
○ s

13.
○ m
○ n
○ l

14.
○ t
○ f
○ r

15.
○ v
○ u
○ r

16.
○ s
○ x
○ c

Final Consonants

Directions: Change the ending sound of the underlined word to complete each sentence. Use the correct word from the word box.

1. The <u>cat</u> ate from a _____.

2. The <u>bug</u> sat on a _____.

3. The <u>pig</u> fell into a _____.

4. The <u>sheep</u> slept in a _____.

5. The <u>rat</u> quickly _____.

6. The <u>man</u> walked on a _____.

7. The <u>dog</u> had a black _____.

8. The <u>kid</u> was his _____.

bud
mat
can
bag
kin
dot
sheet
pit
ran

Final Consonants

Directions: Change the letters that make the ending sound to make new words. Write the new words on the lines.

1. Change	ban	to	
2. Change	her	to	
3. Change	cab	to	
4. Change	fit	to	
5. Change	fat	to	
6. Change	rut	to	
7. Change	kit	to	
8. Change	ton	to	

Initial and Final Consonants

Directions: Say the name for each picture below. Print the letter for its beginning sound and then its ending sound. Then trace the whole word.

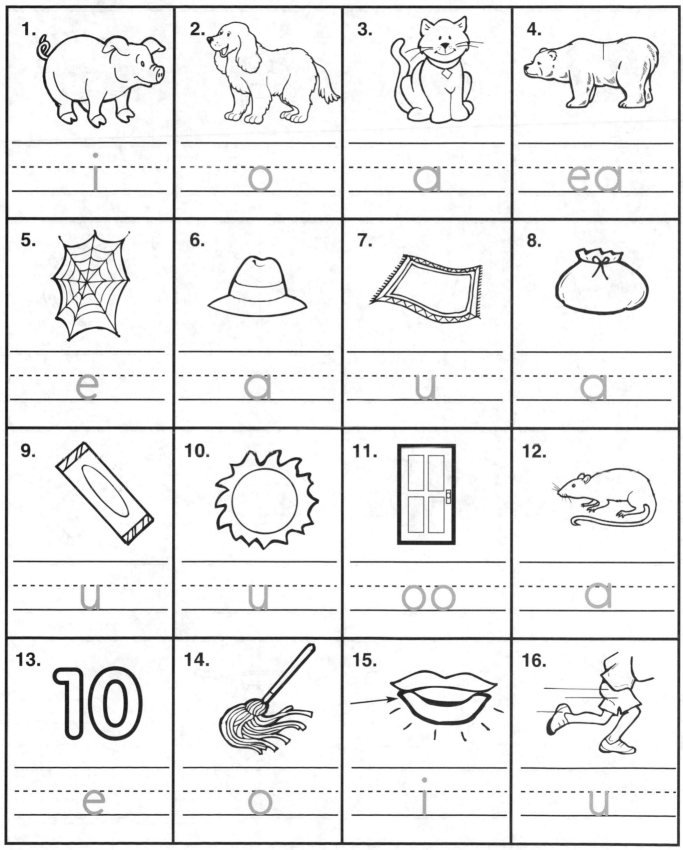

1. i
2. o
3. a
4. ea
5. e
6. a
7. u
8. a
9. u
10. u
11. oo
12. a
13. e
14. o
15. i
16. u

Initial and Final Consonants

Directions: Say the name for each picture below. Print the letter for its beginning sound and then its ending sound. Then trace the whole word.

Medial Consonants

Directions: Say the name for each picture below. Print the letter for its middle consonant sound.

1.

2.

3.

4.

5.

6.

7.

8.

9.

10.

11.

12.

13.

14.

15.

16.

Medial Consonants

Directions: Say the name of each picture below. Print the letter for its middle consonant sound and then trace the whole word.

1. dra_on

2. la_a

3. bu_es

4. ro_ot

5. spi_er

6. se_en

7. le_on

8. ca_el

9. ti_er

10. pea_ut

Medial Consonants

Directions: Say the name for each picture below. Fill in the bubble beside the letter that makes the middle sound in each word.

1. ○ g ○ b ○ d

2. ○ f ○ t ○ s

3. ○ t ○ l ○ f

4. ○ j ○ g ○ t

5. ○ r ○ v ○ t

6. ○ v ○ m ○ n

7. ○ t ○ m ○ l

8. ○ p ○ b ○ r

9. ○ g ○ w ○ n

10. ○ t ○ n ○ b

11. ○ l ○ r ○ t

12. ○ n ○ b ○ s

13. ○ m ○ t ○ l

14. ○ l ○ f ○ r

15. ○ t ○ b ○ r

16. ○ d ○ t ○ l

Medial Consonants

Directions: Read the sentences below. Print the letter for each middle sound and trace the whole word. Do what the sentences tell you to do.

1. Draw a purple dra__on .

2. Draw a yellow __le__on .

3. Draw an orange __ti__er .

4. Draw a blue ro__ot .

5. Draw a brown ru__er .

6. Draw a pink flo__er .

7. Make a red se__en .

8. Draw a black spi__er .

Initial, Medial, and Final Consonants

Directions: Unscramble the letters to the left. Then write the word on the correct line under its picture.

dgo

nus

rgu

bwe

anc

tpo

naf

tar

Initial, Medial, and Final Consonants

Directions: Begin at the top and change letters to make new words as you go down. Write the new words on the lines.

1. Change the **d** in *dog* to **l**.

_____

2. Change the **g** to **t**.

_____

3. Change the **l** to **h**.

_____

4. Change the **o** to **i**.

_____

5. Change the **h** to **b**.

_____

6. Change the **i** to **a**.

_____

7. Change the **b** to **c**.

_____

8. Change the **c** to **r**.

_____

Initial, Medial, and Final Consonants

Directions: Read each sentence below. Use the mixed-up letters in the box to the right to make a word completing the sentence. Write the word on the line.

1. Julie went on the school _____ .	sub
2. The sun was _____ .	toh
3. She used a _____ to cool herself.	anf
4. Julie had a _____ of soda.	nac
5. She liked to _____ the ball.	hti
6. Julie also loved to _____ .	atb
7. Julie had a yellow _____ .	gdo
8. Sue has a black _____ .	tca

Initial, Medial, and Final Consonants

Directions: Start with the word written inside the car. Follow the directions on the right to change a letter to make a new word. Write the new word on the correct line. Write the last word inside the finish line.

car

1. _____   8. _____

2. _____   9. _____

3. _____   10. _____

4. _____   11. _____

5. _____   12. _____

6. _____   13. _____

| **FINISH LINE** |
| 14. _____ |

7. _____

| 1. Change the c to b. |
| 2. Change the r to g. |
| 3. Change the b to t. |
| 4. Change the g to p. |
| 5. Change the a to o. |
| 6. Change the t to c. |
| 7. Change the o to a. |
| 8. Change the p to t. |
| 9. Change the a to u. |
| 10. Change the u to o. |
| 11. Change the c to p. |
| 12. Change the p to h. |
| 13. Change the t to p. |
| 14. Change the h to t. |

Initial, Medial, and Final Consonants

Directions: Write a story about your friends. Use some of the words in the box below. Then illustrate your story.

_____

- -

_____

_____

- -

_____

_____

- -

_____

_____

- -

_____

_____

- -

_____

school	friends	**Illustration**
bus	play	
swing	slide	
ladder	hop	
skip	run	
girls	boys	
teacher	read	

Unit Review

Directions: Circle the word that belongs in the sentence and print it on the correct line.

1. The _____ says oink.	pog pig pan
2. The _____ rings loudly.	ball bell bail
3. The _____ lays eggs.	hand heed hen
4. The _____ likes to sleep.	dog dig dip
5. The _____ gives milk.	cat calf cow
6. I blow bubbles with my _____.	gun gone gum
7. The _____ is for her.	dress drive drain
8. She sleeps in a _____.	bad bend bed

Unit Review

Directions: Say the name of each picture. Fill in the bubble beside the letter for the <u>beginning</u> sound in the word.

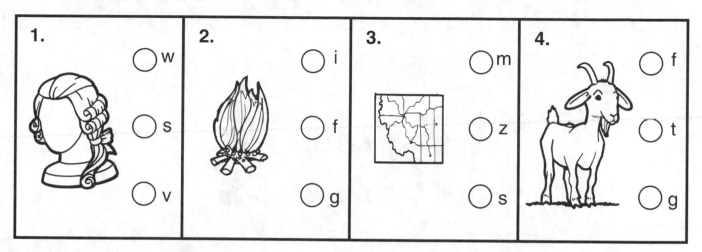

1. ○ w ○ s ○ v

2. ○ i ○ f ○ g

3. ○ m ○ z ○ s

4. ○ f ○ t ○ g

Directions: Say the name of each picture. Fill in the bubble beside the letter for the <u>ending</u> sound in the word.

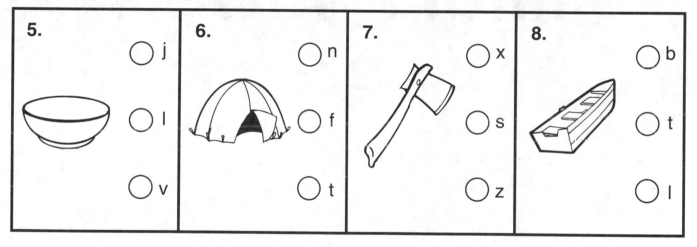

5. ○ j ○ l ○ v

6. ○ n ○ f ○ t

7. ○ x ○ s ○ z

8. ○ b ○ t ○ l

Directions: Say the name of each picture. Fill in the bubble beside the letter for the <u>middle</u> consonant sound in the word.

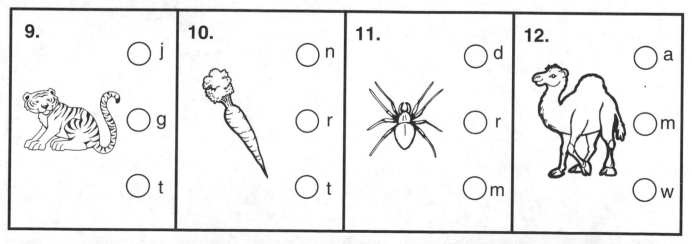

9. ○ j ○ g ○ t

10. ○ n ○ r ○ t

11. ○ d ○ r ○ m

12. ○ a ○ m ○ w

UNIT 2
Short Vowels

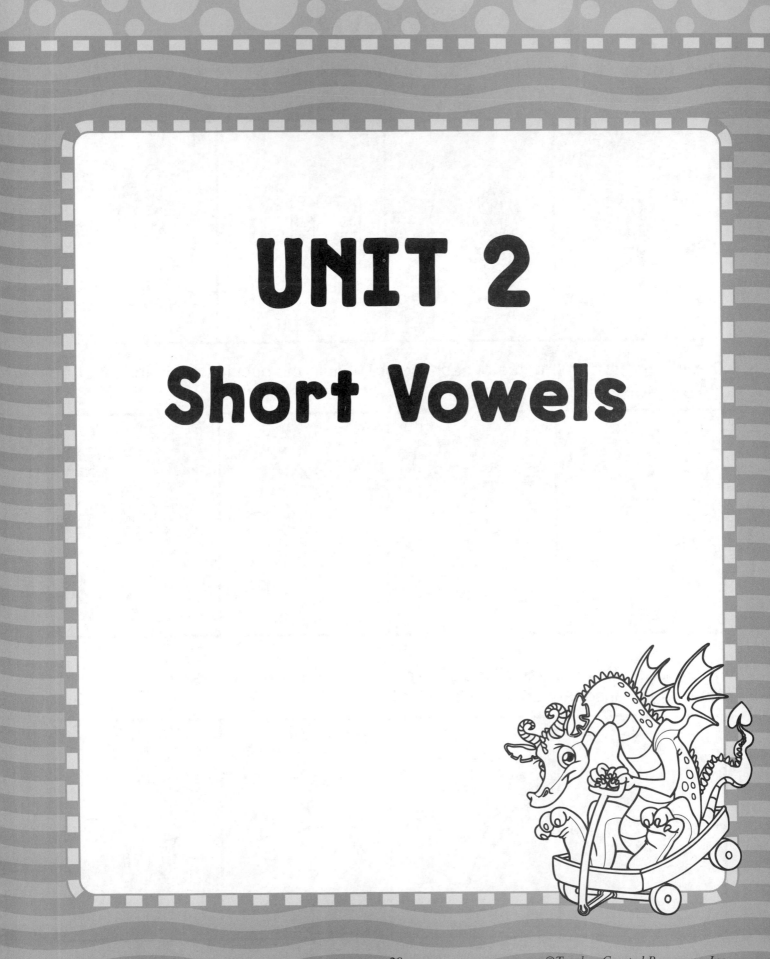

28

Short a

Directions: Say the name of each picture. Circle its name.

RULE

If a word or syllable has only one vowel, and it comes at the beginning or between two consonants, the vowel is usually short. The word *cat* has the short **a** sound.

1.
can
cat
cap
cab

2.
tan
vat
pat
van

3.
dab
pad
dad
did

4.
back
sack
sat
sad

5.
ham
him
hat
had

6.
tat
tan
tap
tag

7.
band
ban
bat
bag

8.
fan
fast
fad
fat

9.
pad
pack
pan
pin

10.
sat
sad
sap
sack

Short a

Directions: Say the name of each picture. Write its name.

1.

2.

3.

4.

5.

6.

7.

8.

9.

10.

11.

12.

Short a

Directions: Write rhyming words in each box. To make rhymes just change the beginning consonant.

cat	**pan**
vat	tan
sad	**cab**
dad	jab

Short i

Directions: Say the name of each picture. Circle its name.

RULE

If a word or syllable has only one vowel, and it comes at the beginning or between two consonants, the vowel is usually short. The word *dig* has the short **i** sound.

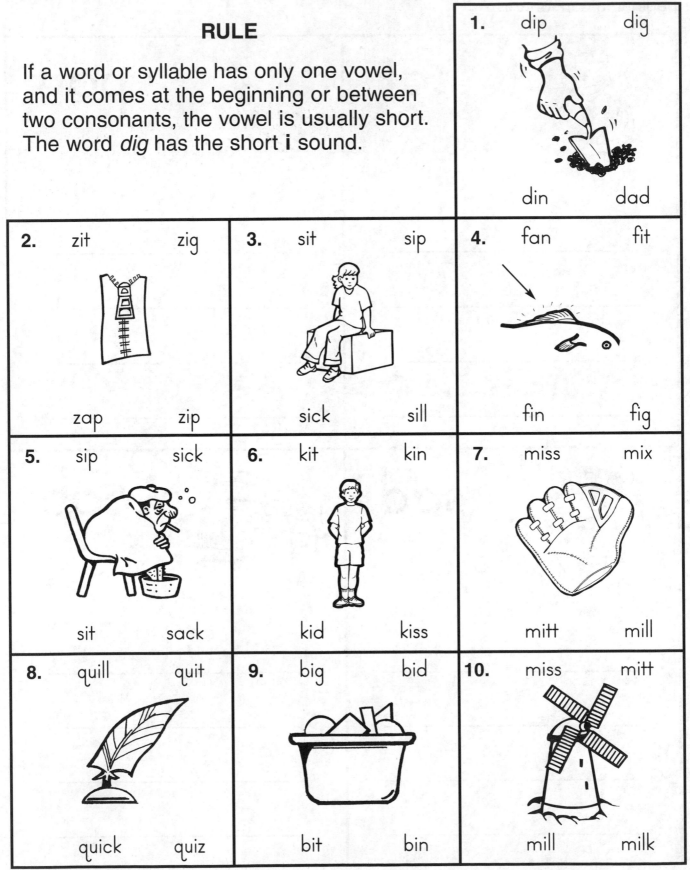

1. dip   dig
   din   dad

2. zit   zig
   zap   zip

3. sit   sip
   sick   sill

4. fan   fit
   fin   fig

5. sip   sick
   sit   sack

6. kit   kin
   kid   kiss

7. miss   mix
   mitt   mill

8. quill   quit
   quick   quiz

9. big   bid
   bit   bin

10. miss   mitt
    mill   milk

Short i

Directions: Say the name of each picture. Write its name.

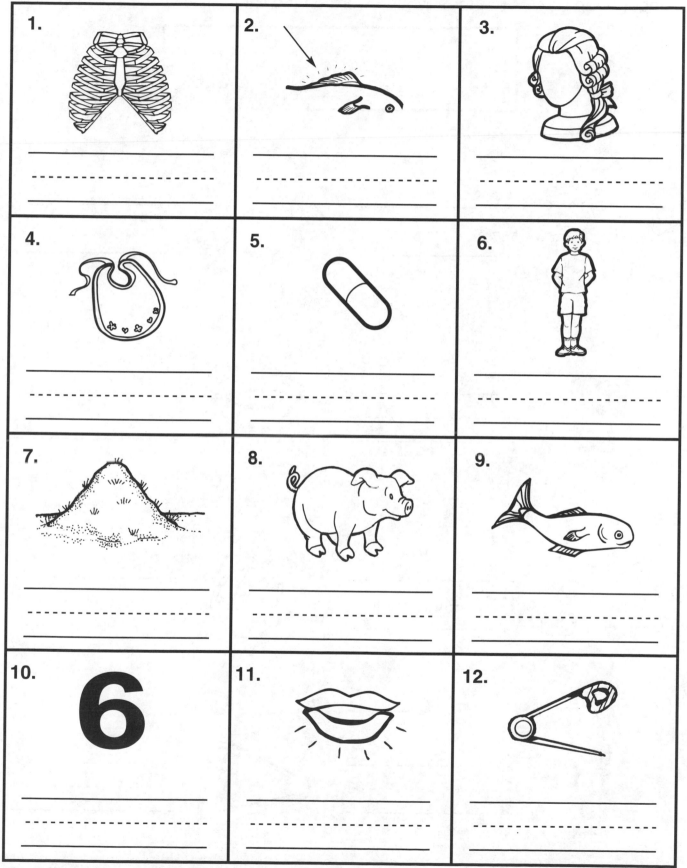

1.

2.

3.

4.

5.

6.

7.

8.

9.

10.

11.

12.

Short i

Directions: Say the name of each picture. Find a rhyming word for the picture in the top box. Write the rhyming word on the line.

tin	fix	fib	him
rid	pip	wig	wish

1.

2.

3.

6

4.

5.

6.

7.

8.

Short u

Directions: Say the name of each picture. Circle its name.

RULE

If a word or syllable has only one vowel, and it comes at the beginning or between two consonants, the vowel is usually short. The word *cub* has the short **u** sound.

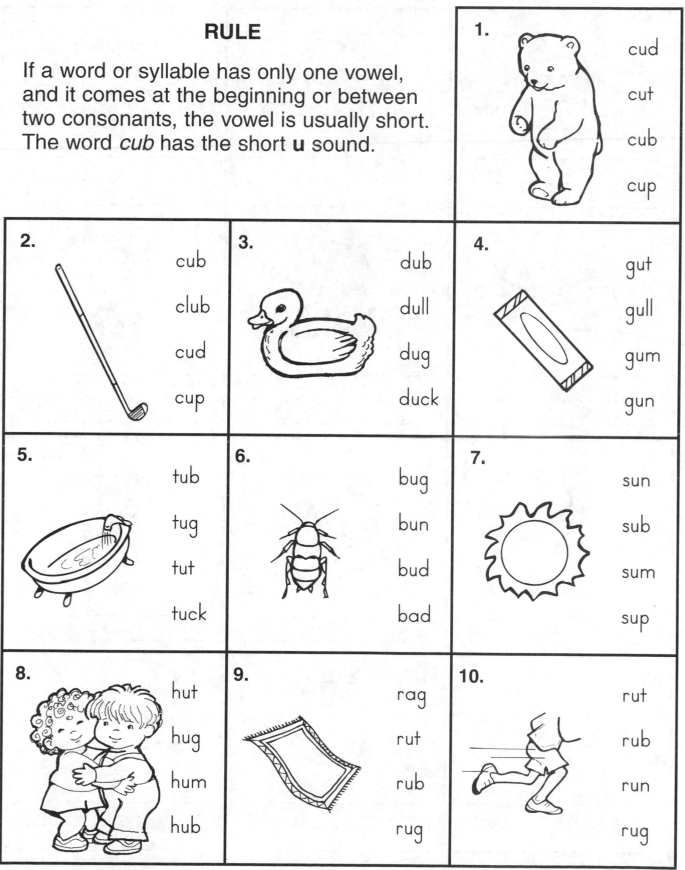

1.

cud

cut

cub

cup

2.

cub

club

cud

cup

3.

dub

dull

dug

duck

4.

gut

gull

gum

gun

5.

tub

tug

tut

tuck

6.

bug

bun

bud

bad

7.

sun

sub

sum

sup

8.

hut

hug

hum

hub

9.

rag

rut

rub

rug

10.

rut

rub

run

rug

Short u

Directions: Say the name of each picture. Write its name

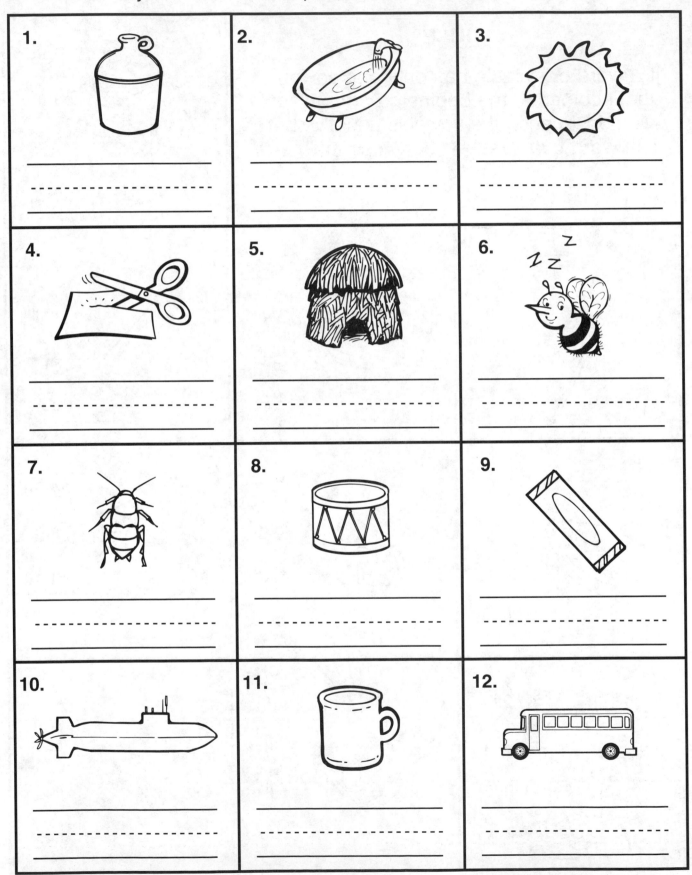

1.

2.

3.

4.

5.

6.

7.

8.

9.

10.

11.

12.

Short u

Directions: Make new rhymes by changing the first consonant. Use the consonant that is in the box at the beginning of the row.

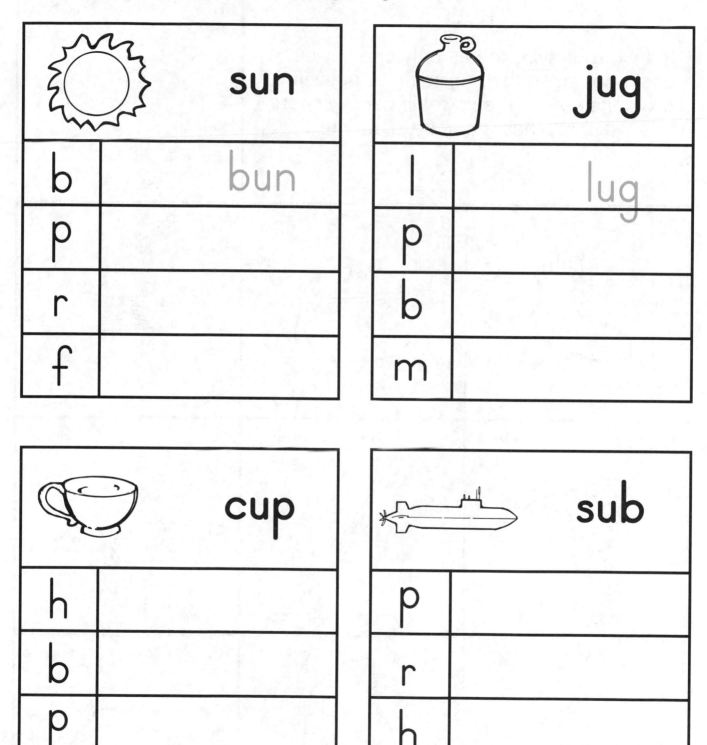

	sun
b	bun
p	
r	
f	

	jug
l	lug
p	
b	
m	

	cup
h	
b	
p	
s	

	sub
p	
r	
h	
t	

Short o

Directions: Say the name of each picture. Circle its name.

RULE

If a word or syllable has only one vowel, and it comes at the beginning or between two consonants, the vowel is usually short. The word *hop* has the short **o** sound.

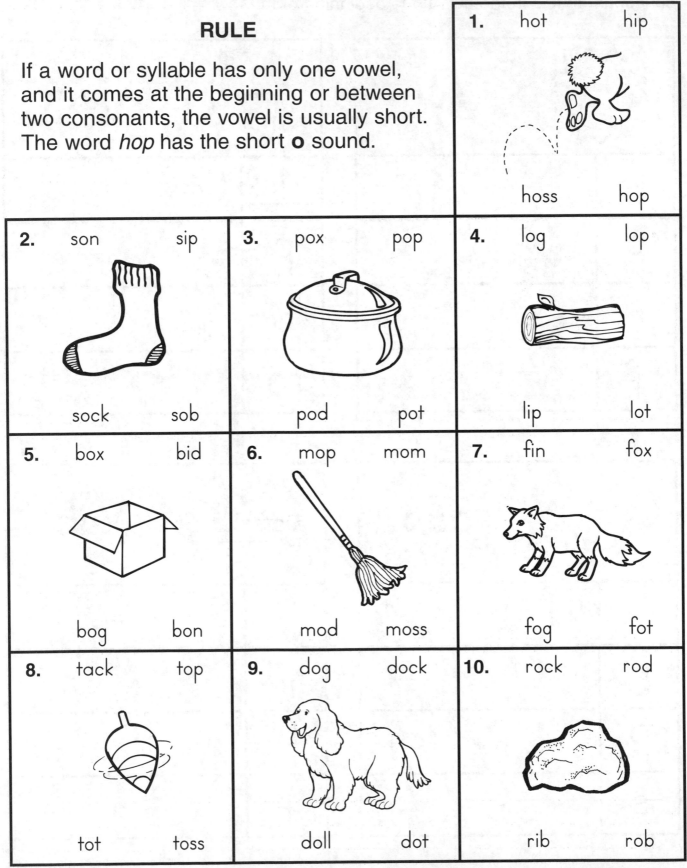

1. hot — hip hoss — hop		
2. son — sip sock — sob	**3.** pox — pop pod — pot	**4.** log — lop lip — lot
5. box — bid bog — bon	**6.** mop — mom mod — moss	**7.** fin — fox fog — fot
8. tack — top tot — toss	**9.** dog — dock doll — dot	**10.** rock — rod rib — rob

Short o

Directions: Say the name of each picture. Write its name.

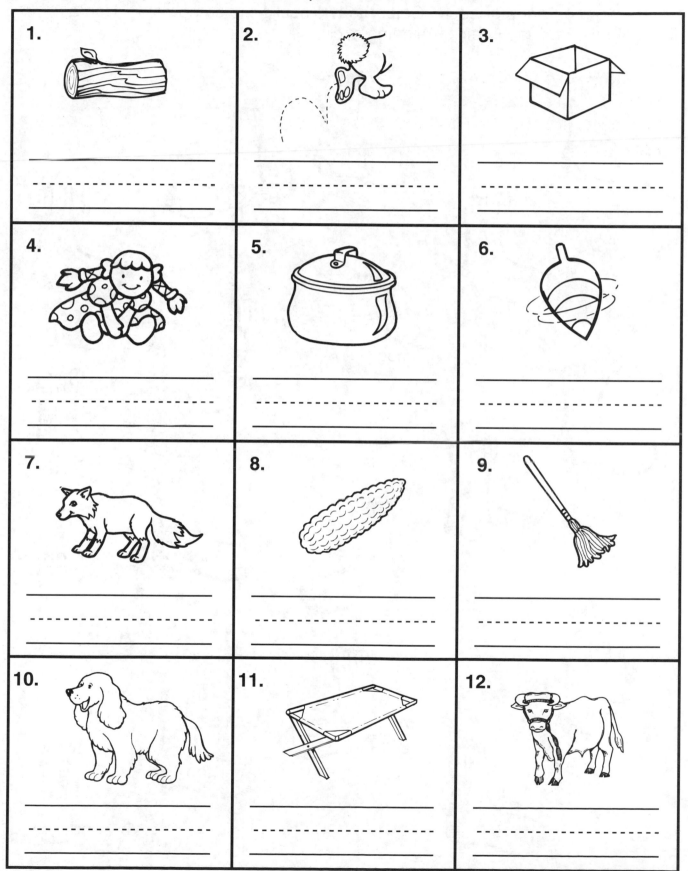

1.

2.

3.

4.

5.

6.

7.

8.

9.

10.

11.

12.

Short o

Directions: Match the socks. Read the word on a sock. Find the rhyming word for that word on another sock. Color the two socks the same color. Use a different color for each pair of rhyming socks.

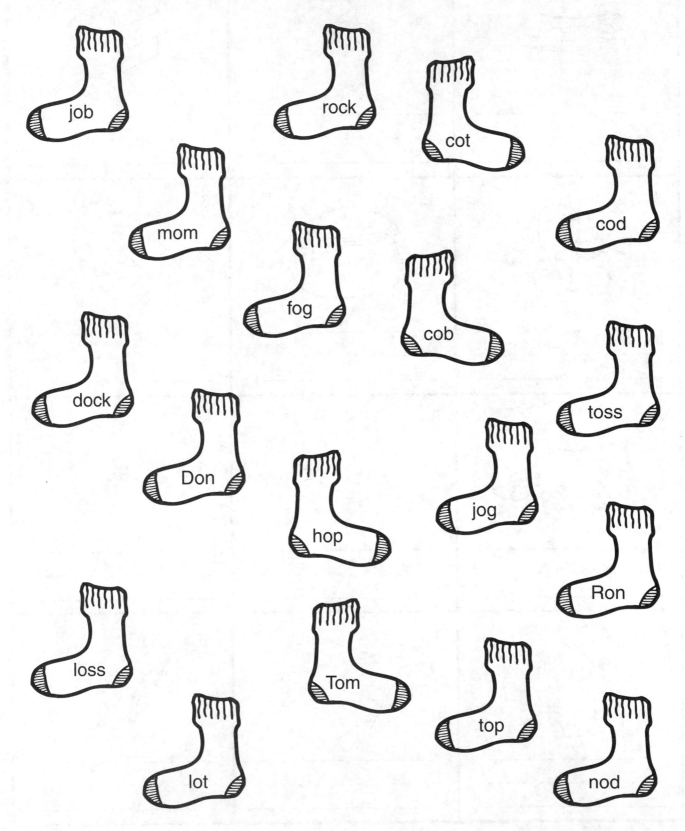

Short e

Directions: Say the name of each picture. Circle its name.

RULE

If a word or syllable has only one vowel, and it comes at the beginning or between two consonants, the vowel is usually short. The word *web* has the short **e** sound.

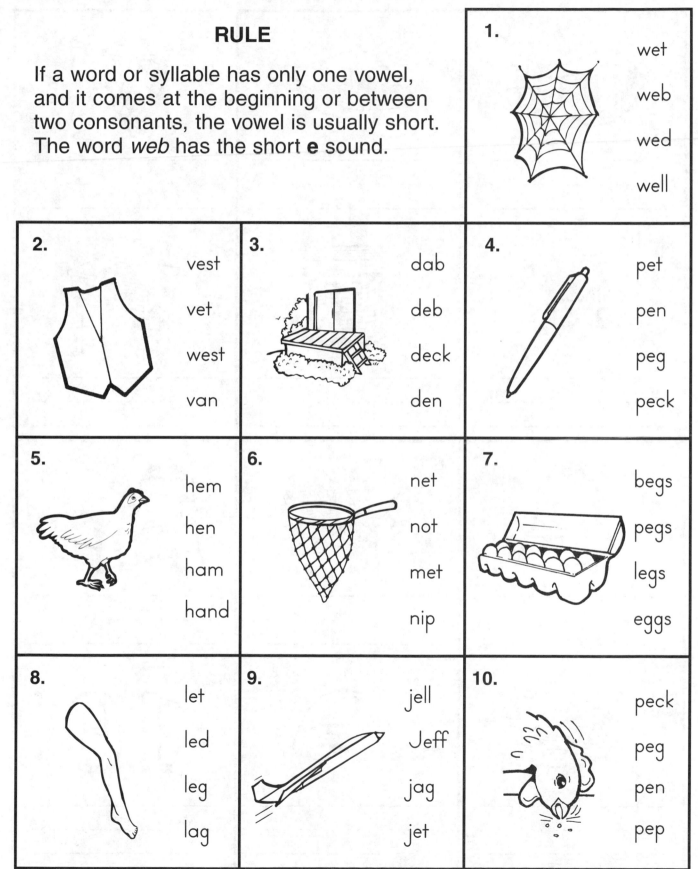

1.

wet

web

wed

well

2.

vest

vet

west

van

3.

dab

deb

deck

den

4.

pet

pen

peg

peck

5.

hem

hen

ham

hand

6.

net

not

met

nip

7.

begs

pegs

legs

eggs

8.

let

led

leg

lag

9.

jell

Jeff

jag

jet

10.

peck

peg

pen

pep

Short e

Directions: Say the name of each picture. Write its name.

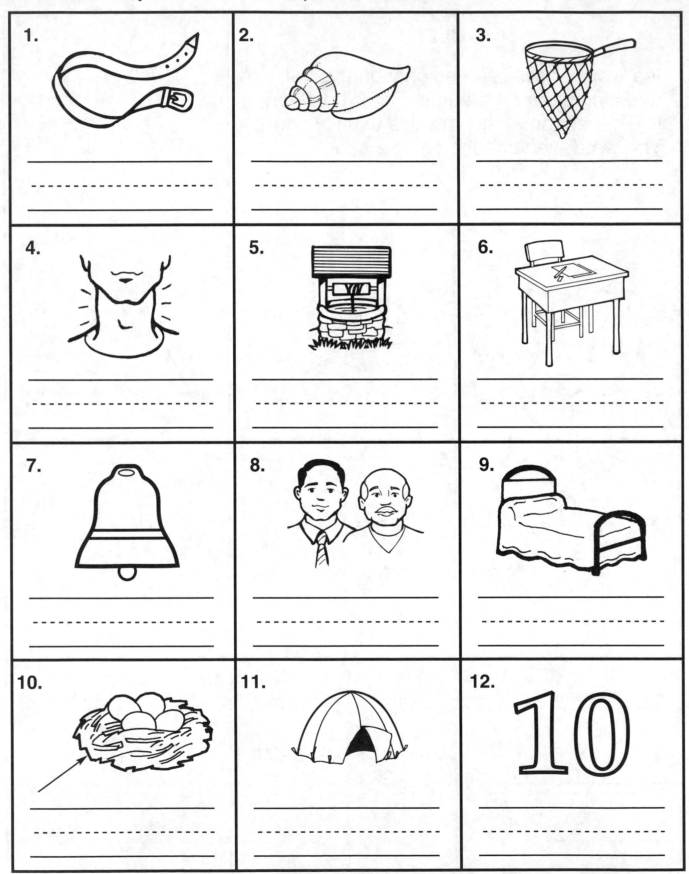

1.

2.

3.

4.

5.

6.

7.

8.

9.

10.

11.

12.

Short e

Directions: Complete the crossword puzzle by writing the short **e** words in the correct places. Use the words at the bottom of the page to help you.

Across ➡

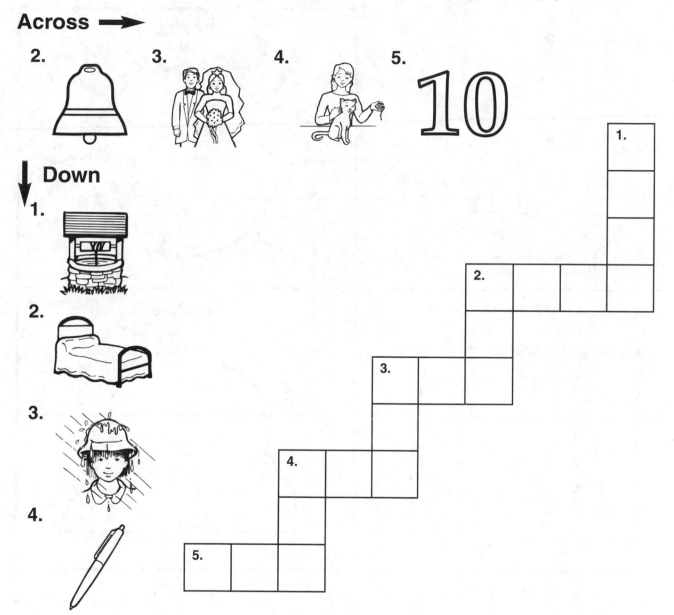

Down ⬇

Directions: Trace the rhyming words.

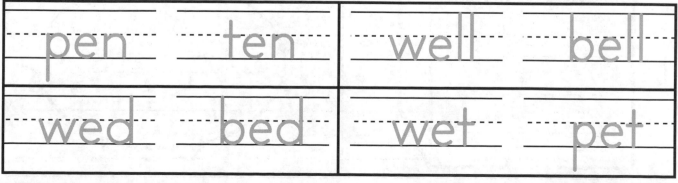

Short Vowels

Directions: Read the words in the list. Write each word in the shape that matches the short vowel sound in the word.

loss   sell   rap

hip   fuss   bid

pod   ram   pit

yet   dug   led

job   gap   bud

short u

short a

short e

short o

short i

Short Vowels

Directions: Read each riddle. Circle the answer.

1. It has five fingers. What is it?

band   hand

hat   land

2. It is on a fish. What is it?

fan   fun

fin   win

3. Kids ride it to school. What is it?

bus   buck

bun   bug

4. I play with her. What is it?

dill   dot

dull   doll

5. I sleep on it. What is it?

bell   bed

bad   bet

6. It rhymes with sock. What is it?

rod   rob

rock   rot

7. It can hit a ball. What is it?

bat   bet

bag   ban

8. It can lay an egg. What is it?

pen   hand

hem   hen

9. It goes quack. What is it?

deck   dock

duck   luck

Short Vowels

Directions: Read each sentence. Fill in the bubble beside the sentence that tells about the picture.

1.

◯ The cat is on the mat.

◯ The cat is on the sill.

◯ The cat is not on the sill.

◯ The cat is in the box.

2.

◯ The frog is under the lily pad.

◯ The frog is not on the lily pad.

◯ The frog is on the lily pad.

◯ The frog is in a pot.

3.

◯ The bug sat on a rock.

◯ The bug is not in the net.

◯ The dog is in the net.

◯ The bug is in the net.

4.

◯ The pig is in the pen.

◯ The pig is not in the pen.

◯ The cat is in the pen.

◯ The pig is on the mat.

5.

◯ The dog sat in the sun.

◯ The cub ran in the sun.

◯ The dog ran in the sun.

◯ The dog is in a jet.

Short Vowels

Directions: Read each sentence. Circle the word that completes the sentence and write it on the line.

	1. This is Pam. She is my _____ .	sit sis sill
	2. We like to run and _____ .	hop hot hock
	3. Mom and Dad gave us a _____ .	pip puff pup
	4. We call him _____ .	Bag Bob Bat
	5. Pam got him to sit up and _____ .	beg bag ban
	6. He likes to nap on my _____ .	bell bet bed
	7. He can jump over a _____ .	lot log lock
	8. He is a lot of _____ !	fuss fix fun

Short Vowels

Directions: Read the story and then answer the questions.

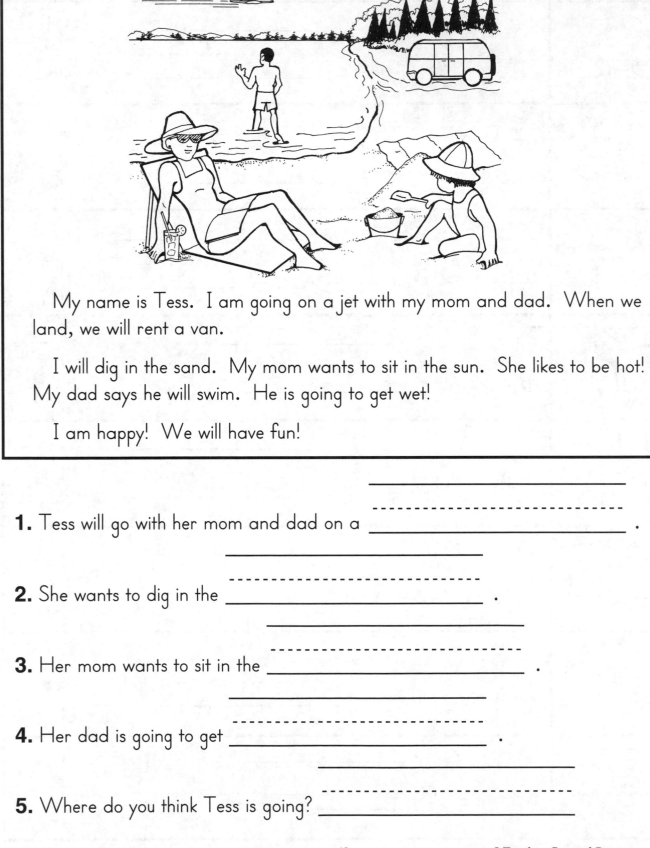

My name is Tess. I am going on a jet with my mom and dad. When we land, we will rent a van.

I will dig in the sand. My mom wants to sit in the sun. She likes to be hot! My dad says he will swim. He is going to get wet!

I am happy! We will have fun!

1. Tess will go with her mom and dad on a _____ .

2. She wants to dig in the _____ .

3. Her mom wants to sit in the _____ .

4. Her dad is going to get _____ .

5. Where do you think Tess is going? _____

Short Vowels

Directions: Read each sentence. Write **yes** if it is true. Write **no** if it is not true.

1. I can sip from a cup.	_____
2. A jet must be red.	_____
3. A hen can swim.	_____
4. A man can drive a van.	_____
5. He is six. Next, he will be ten.	_____
6. A fish has a fin.	_____
7. A bell can run.	_____
8. A pig can play in the mud.	_____
9. A cat likes to be wet.	_____
10. An ant plays with a doll.	_____
11. A fox will live in a den.	_____
12. I can nap on a cot.	_____

Unit Review

Directions: Say the name of the picture. Circle the letter that matches the short vowel sound.

1. a e i o u
2. a e i o u
3. a e i o u
4. a e i o u

5. a e i o u
6. a e i o u
7. a e i o u
8. a e i o u

9. a e i o u
10. a e i o u
11. a e i o u
12. a e i o u

13. a e i o u
14. a e i o u
15. a e i o u
16. a e i o u

Unit Review

Directions: Pick a word from the box that will finish the sentence. Print it on the line. Use each word one time.

1. Ten men are on the _____ .

2. Be sure to turn the _____ .

3. I want to eat this _____ .

4. I have a dog for a _____ .

5. I see a pig that is _____ .

6. He cut the log with an _____ .

7. I fell into the _____ .

8. My mom gave me a _____ .

9. The fat cat sat in my _____ .

10. At his job he is the _____ .

11. I can hear the _____ .

kiss

pet

boss

lock

mud

jet

lap

big

bell

ax

bun

UNIT 3
Long Vowels

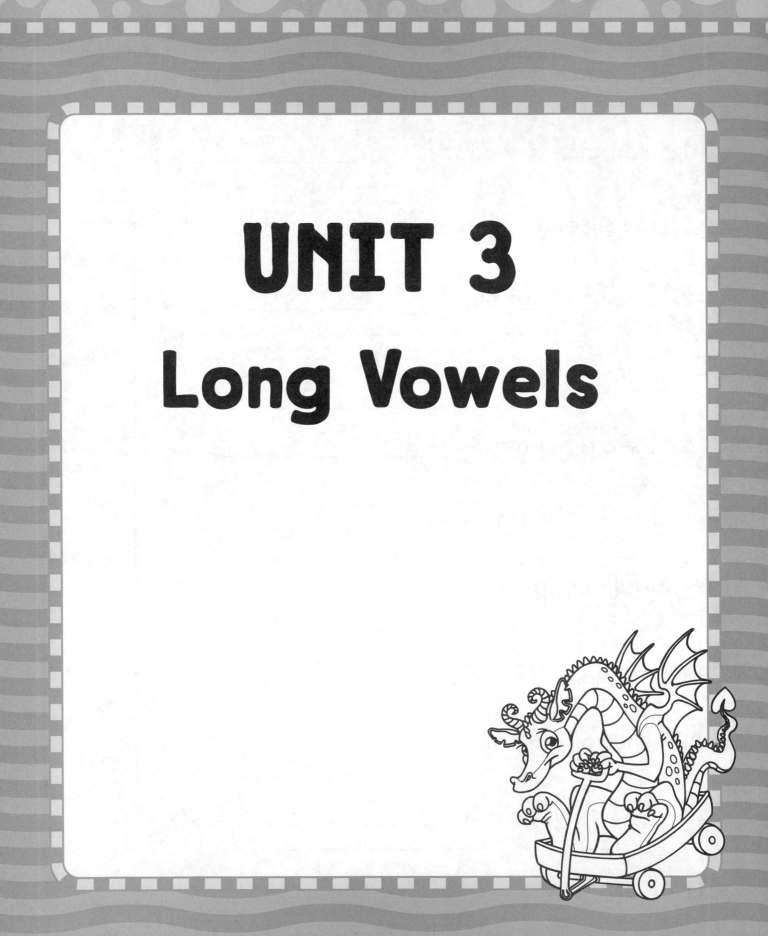

Long a

Directions: Print the long **a** words in the boxes below to name each picture.

RULE

If a word or syllable has two vowels, the first vowel usually makes a long sound, and the second is silent.

cake	rake	tape	gate	plane	May
mail	rain	wave	play	game	tray

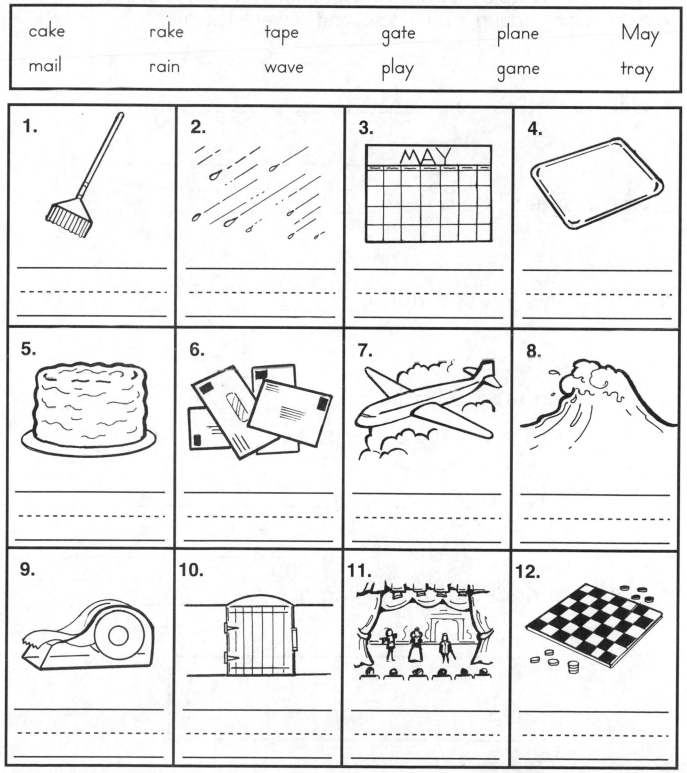

1.

2.

3.

4.

5.

6.

7.

8.

9.

10.

11.

12.

Long a

Directions: You can hear the long **a** sound in *plane*, *rain*, and *rave*. Find the long **a** word in the box below that will finish each sentence. Then print it on the line.

RULE

If a word or syllable has two vowels, the first vowel is usually makes a long sound, and the second vowel is silent.

1. Jill wanted to go _____ outside.

2. She wanted to play with _____ .

3. They loved to play fun _____ .

4. Jill's friend Jake had a toy air_____ .

5. The friends played all _____ .

6. Let's go inside. It is starting to _____ .

Jane	play	day
plane	games	rain

Long i

Directions: Print the long **i** words in the boxes below to name each picture.

RULE

If a word or syllable has two vowels, the first vowel usually makes a long sound, and the second vowel is silent.

bike	kite	hike	timer	tide	ride
dime	pine	tie	mice	ice	lime

1.

2.

3.

4.

5.

6.

7.

8.

9.

10.

11.

12.

Long i and Short i

Directions: You can hear the long **i** sound in *bike, ride,* and *hide*. Print the short **i** words under the Short Vowel Sound column and the long **i** words under the Long Vowel Sound column.

RULE

If a word or syllable has two vowels, the first vowel usually makes a long sound, and the second vowel is silent.

bite	bit	ride	hide	sit	side	slide
tide	bid	rid	wipe	whip	six	sick

Short Vowel Sound	Long Vowel Sound

Long a and Long i

Directions: Read each sentence below. Circle the word that makes sense and print it on the line.

1. The _____ flies in the wind.	cake	kite	kiln
2. The _____ is for Jack's birthday.	cake	bill	bake
3. The fox has a bushy _____.	till	tail	toe
4. Ten cents is worth a _____.	time	rhyme	dime
5. An umbrella is good to have in the _____.	rain	rail	rate
6. The boy likes to ride on a _____.	bile	bike	bit
7. She drove the car for one _____.	rail	mail	mile
8. He likes to _____ his pictures.	pant	pint	paint
9. The clock tells the correct _____.	tame	time	taint

Long o

Directions: Print the long **o** words in the boxes below to name each picture.

RULE

If a word or syllable has two vowels, the first vowel usually makes a long sound, and the second vowel is silent.

coat	goat	boat	bone	nose	hose
rose	road	soap	rope	notes	joker

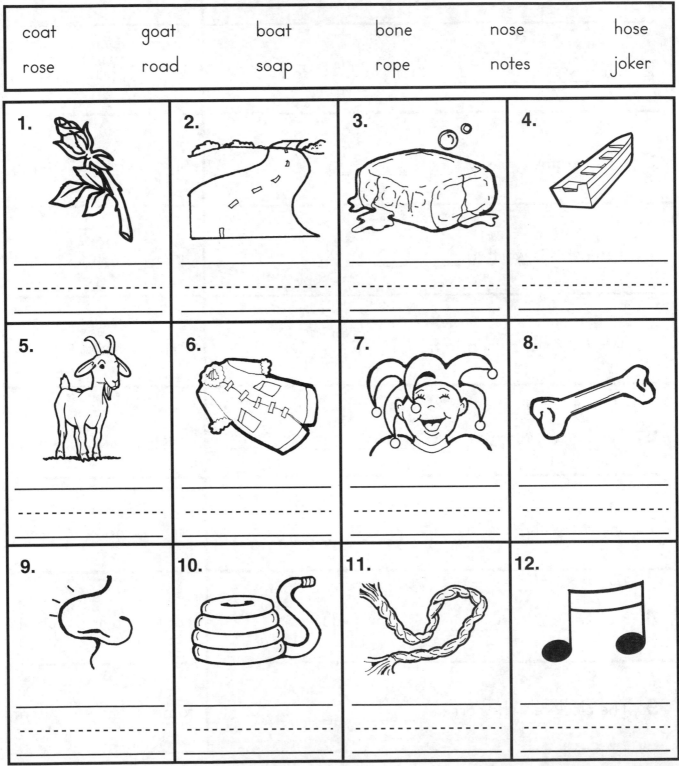

1.

2.

3.

4.

5.

6.

7.

8.

9.

10.

11.

12.

Long o

Directions: You can hear the long **o** sound in *no, troll,* and *goat.* Find the long **o** words in the box below that will finish each sentence. Then print it on the line.

RULE

If a word or syllable has two vowels, the first vowel usually makes a long sound, and the second vowel is silent.

1. Noel _____ a dog.

2. The dog's name was _____ .

3. He liked to chew on a big _____ .

4. He was always happy for one in his _____ .

5. Joe liked to bury his bones in a _____ .

6. When he was done, he would have dirt on his _____ .

bone	Joe	bowl
nose	owned	hole

Long u

Directions: Print the long **u** words in the boxes below to name each picture.

RULE

If a word or syllable has two vowels, the first vowel usually makes a long sound, and the second vowel is silent.

tube	flute	suit	glue	fruit	ruler
clue	mule	cube	June	bugle	music

1.

2.

3.

4.

5.

6.

7.

8.

9.

10.

11.

12.

60 ©Teacher Created Resources, Inc.

Long u

Directions: You can hear the long **u** sound in *tube*, *suit*, and *flute*. Fill in the bubble in front of the long **u** word that will finish each sentence. Then print the word on the line.

1. Julie likes to play the _____ .	◯ fuel ◯ flute
2. June likes to play in _____ .	◯ tune ◯ tone
3. Sue loves to play the _____ .	◯ lute ◯ late
4. Jude plays the _____ .	◯ bug ◯ bugle
5. Rudy plays the _____ .	◯ tuba ◯ tub
6. Ruby loves their _____ .	◯ music ◯ mud
7. Judy likes to _____ Jewel's drums.	◯ use ◯ us
8. She had to fix the sticks with _____ .	◯ glue ◯ gun
9. They were a bright _____ color.	◯ blue ◯ bay
10. Raul was home with the _____ .	◯ flu ◯ fun

Long o and Long u

Directions: Read each sentence below. Circle the word that makes sense and print it on the line.

1. She washed her hands with _____ .	soup soap soot
2. She used the _____ of toothpaste.	tube tool toad
3. The man _____ his new car.	drove dove dog
4. She sang the high _____ beautifully.	not nut note
5. The cowboy used his _____ for the trick.	rut rope ripe
6. She played the _____ in the concert.	flat flute float
7. Her drink had a lot of ice _____ .	cubs cooks cubes
8. The sky is very _____ today.	blue blow bloat
9. She plays _____ on the piano.	moose music muse
10. She _____ a letter to her friend.	wrote rope write

Long e

Directions: Print the long **e** word in each box below to name each picture.

RULE

If a word or syllable has two vowels, the first vowel usually makes a long sound, and the second vowel is silent.

bee	tree	three	beet	feet	eat
seat	pea	jeans	bead	seal	jeep

1.

2.

3.

4.

5.

6.

7.

8.

9.

10.

11.

12.

Long e

Directions: You can hear the long **e** sound in *feet, beet,* and *street.* Use some of the long **e** words in the box below to write a story.

RULE

If a word or syllable has two vowels, the first vowel usually makes a long sound, and the second vowel is silent.

Keith	Jean	feet	street	weep	seat
sweep	jeep	beans	beak	seen	east

Long e, Long i, and Long o

Directions: Read each word in the box below. Print the word under the correct column.

feet	kite	boat	pine	choke	goat	hike
street	coat	bike	bite	broke	site	rope
side	nine	east	Easter	mile	mole	meal
dime	free	bile	pie	seen	bead	cope

Long e	Long i	Long o

Long e, Long a, and Long u

Directions: Write a story about your school. Use as many words from the box that you can. Then draw a picture of your school.

street	day	blue	teacher
rule	seat	free	week
take	say	cube	mail

_____

- -

_____

_____

- -

_____

_____

- -

_____

_____

- -

_____

_____

- -

_____

My School

Long and Short Vowels

Directions: Say the name of each picture below. Print the vowel sound that you hear on the line. If the vowel is short, fill in the bubble labeled **short**. If the vowel is long, fill in the bubble labeled **long**.

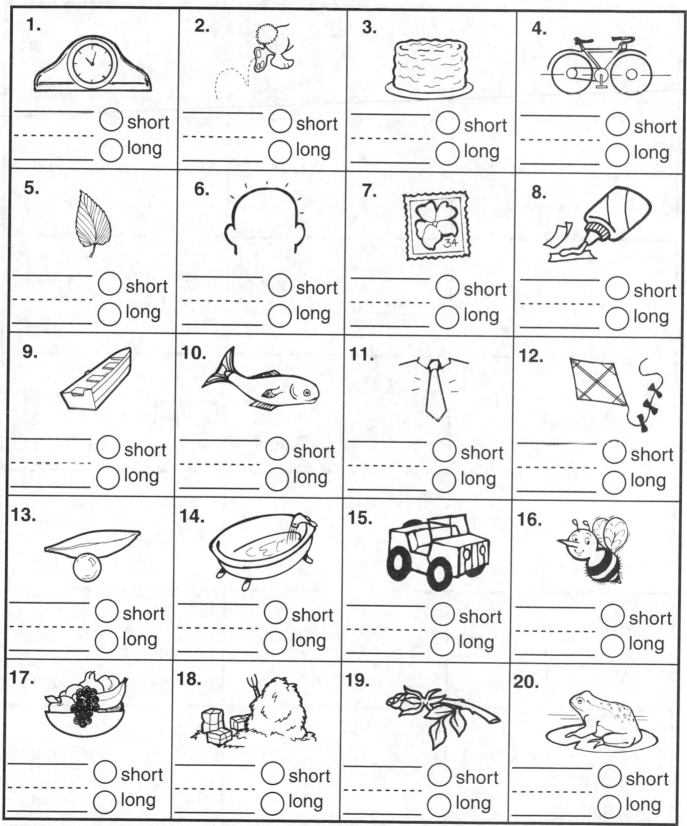

1. _____ ○ short ○ long
2. _____ ○ short ○ long
3. _____ ○ short ○ long
4. _____ ○ short ○ long
5. _____ ○ short ○ long
6. _____ ○ short ○ long
7. _____ ○ short ○ long
8. _____ ○ short ○ long
9. _____ ○ short ○ long
10. _____ ○ short ○ long
11. _____ ○ short ○ long
12. _____ ○ short ○ long
13. _____ ○ short ○ long
14. _____ ○ short ○ long
15. _____ ○ short ○ long
16. _____ ○ short ○ long
17. _____ ○ short ○ long
18. _____ ○ short ○ long
19. _____ ○ short ○ long
20. _____ ○ short ○ long

Long and Short Vowels

Directions: Read each word below. If the word has a long vowel, fill in the bubble in front of the word **long**. If the word has a short vowel, fill in the bubble in front of the word **short**.

1. date ○ short ○ long	**2.** tune ○ short ○ long	**3.** fuel ○ short ○ long
4. fan ○ short ○ long	**5.** tube ○ short ○ long	**6.** hide ○ short ○ long
7. train ○ short ○ long	**8.** sick ○ short ○ long	**9.** box ○ short ○ long
10. fuse ○ short ○ long	**11.** cute ○ short ○ long	**12.** sap ○ short ○ long
13. gate ○ short ○ long	**14.** chime ○ short ○ long	**15.** sun ○ short ○ long
16. rake ○ short ○ long	**17.** tick ○ short ○ long	**18.** bus ○ short ○ long
19. nap ○ short ○ long	**20.** ride ○ short ○ long	**21.** rate ○ short ○ long

Long and Short Vowels

Directions: Complete the rhyming words below.

1. cat	rat	bat		**11.** cut	h___	b___
2. tent	w___	d___		**12.** wake	b___	c___
3. sun	b___	f___		**13.** pea	s___	t___
4. rate	g___	b___		**14.** mud	b___	d___
5. bike	l___	h___		**15.** bite	k___	s___
6. goat	b___	c___		**16.** pig	w___	f___
7. cap	n___	s___		**17.** rose	n___	h___
8. fit	b___	h___		**18.** top	h___	c___
9. not	h___	c___		**19.** dog	f___	l___
10. meat	h___	b___		**20.** cave	w___	s___

Long and Short Vowels

Directions: Add a second vowel to the words below to make new words.

1. bit _____	**2.** pan _____	**3.** sad _____
4. red _____	**5.** ran _____	**6.** wed _____
7. ton _____	**8.** bat _____	**9.** hop _____
10. con _____	**11.** rat _____	**12.** fat _____

Directions: Take one vowel away from each word below to make new words.

13. cane _____	**14.** pane _____	**15.** rain _____
16. kite _____	**17.** weed _____	**18.** hope _____
19. fine _____	**20.** robe _____	**21.** seat _____
22. bait _____	**23.** cube _____	**24.** tube _____

Long and Short Vowels

Directions: Say each word in the box below. Print the word in the correct column.

kite	net	doll	goat	bed	bag	tube
sock	nine	duck	coat	feet	cub	cube
hat	bike	fish	tack	tail	bean	goes

Long Vowel Sound	Short Vowel Sound

Long Vowels

Directions: Say and spell each long vowel word. Print the word on the road that shows its long vowel sound.

fuse	feet	bay	line	vote
goat	tube	time	mule	seed
tape	white	bean	nail	bow

Long a

_____ _____ _____

Long e

_____ _____ _____

Long i

_____ _____ _____

Long o

_____ _____ _____

Long u

_____ _____ _____

Long Vowels

Directions: Circle the long vowel words in the puzzle below. Use some of the words to write a story.

r	i	e	f	l	o	a	t
b	a	k	e	a	w	p	a
i	e	a	e	a	r	l	c
w	a	i	t	a	i	a	u
a	p	b	o	a	t	t	t
j	e	a	n	s	e	e	e
s	u	i	t	t	o	i	e
a	k	i	t	e	p	e	a

bake
feet
cute
kite
float
wait
pea
suit
write
boat
plate
jeans

Unit Review

Directions: Fill in the bubble in front of the word that will finish each sentence. Then print the word on the line.

1. The birthday _____ was pink.	⭘ make ⭘ crate ⭘ cake
2. The dog is very _____ .	⭘ cute ⭘ cut ⭘ cure
3. The girl's dress is _____ .	⭘ blue ⭘ dule ⭘ blow
4. Tom loves to ride on his _____ .	⭘ like ⭘ drive ⭘ bike
5. Sue likes to eat green _____ .	⭘ jeans ⭘ ban ⭘ beans
6. Sam climbed the red _____ .	⭘ get ⭘ gate ⭘ mate
7. The _____ sailed on the water.	⭘ bat ⭘ coat ⭘ boat
8. The _____ flew in the air.	⭘ kit ⭘ site ⭘ kite
9. Joe had tired _____ .	⭘ tree ⭘ feet ⭘ seek
10. Jane's _____ was black.	⭘ coat ⭘ con ⭘ cope

Unit Review

Directions: Say and spell each long vowel word below. Print the word in the column that is labeled with its long vowel sound.

use	feel	ray	nine	note	boat	lute
time	mule	lead	tape	pie	teen	nail
bow	tube	rain	seat	ride	mail	hope
jeans	hole	train	bike	fuse	take	flute

Long a	Long e	Long i	Long o	Long u

UNIT 4

Compounds, le Words, Hard and Soft c and g, Blends y as a Vowel, Digraphs, and r-Controlled Vowels

Compound Words

Directions: Find two words in each sentence to put together into a compound word to complete the sentence.

RULE

A **compound word** is made up of two or more words joined together. *Popcorn* is made by joining the words *pop* and *corn*.

1. A *house* for a *dog* is a _____ .

2. A *man* made out of *snow* is a _____ .

3. A *shell* from the *sea* is a _____ .

4. A *bird* that is *blue* is a _____ .

5. A *hive* for a *bee* is a _____ .

6. A *bell* for a *door* is a _____ .

7. A *room* for a *bed* is a _____ .

8. A *pot* for *tea* is a _____ .

Syllables

Directions: Say the name of each picture. Write down the number of syllables you hear in each word.

RULE

Most words are made of small parts called **syllables**. Each syllable has one vowel sound. The word *cat* has one syllable and the word *kitten* has two syllables.

Syllables and Compound Words

Directions: Write the number of syllables for each word or compound word. Then use the words to complete the sentences.

_____ hill   _____ games   _____ candles

_____ popcorn   _____ car   _____ backpack

_____ eagle   _____ cabin

1. Come with me to my uncle's _____ .

2. You will need a big _____ .

3. We will climb a huge _____ .

4. We can play _____ .

5. I hope we see an _____ .

6. When it gets dark, we'll light _____ .

7. We will eat cupcakes and _____ .

8. Let's go! I just put gas in the _____ .

Words Ending in le

Directions: Say the name of each picture. Circle its name.

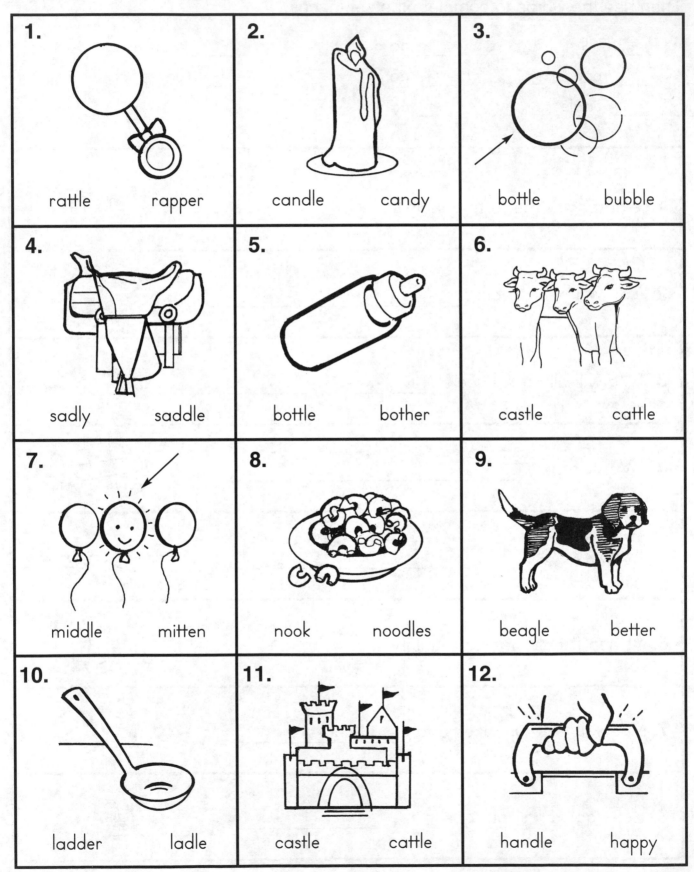

1. rattle   rapper

2. candle   candy

3. bottle   bubble

4. sadly   saddle

5. bottle   bother

6. castle   cattle

7. middle   mitten

8. nook   noodles

9. beagle   better

10. ladder   ladle

11. castle   cattle

12. handle   happy

Hard and Soft c

Directions: Say the name of each picture. If the **c** sound is soft, as in *city*, circle the word **soft**. If the **c** sound is hard, as in *cab*, circle the word **hard**.

RULE

When **c** is followed by **e**, **i**, or **y**, it usually has a soft sound as in *city*. When **c** is followed by **a**, **o**, or **u**, it has a hard sound as in *cab*.

1. hard   soft

city

2. hard   soft

cab

3. hard   soft

camel

4. hard   soft

Cinderella

5. hard   soft

cereal

6. hard   soft

cot

7. hard   soft

dice

8. hard   soft

candy

9. hard   soft

princess

10. hard   soft

cube

11. hard   soft

cannon

12. hard   soft

corn

13. hard   soft

lettuce

14. hard   soft

cymbals

Hard and Soft g

Directions: Say the name of each picture. If the **g** sound is soft, as in *gem*, circle the word **soft**. If the **g** sound is hard, as in *go*, circle the word **hard**.

RULE

When **g** is followed by **e**, **i**, or **y**, it usually has a soft sound as in *gem*. When **g** is followed by **a**, **o**, **u**, it has a hard sound as in *go*.

1. hard   soft

gold

2. hard   soft

magician

3. hard   soft

gingerbread

4. hard   soft

alligator

5. hard   soft

golf

6. hard   soft

gymnastics

7. hard   soft

gypsy

8. hard   soft

garden

9. hard   soft

guitar

10. hard   soft

cabbage

11. hard   soft

gorilla

12. hard   soft

gerbil

13. hard   soft

gem

14. hard   soft

penguin

Hard and Soft c and g

Directions: Read the words. Write each word in the correct box.

cuff	sage	gull	nice	cut	gobble
gym	cast	cent	cob	gap	recess
gust	go	city	cane	barge	ginger
cone	cyst	giant	judge	citrus	gallon

Hard c	Soft c	Hard g	Soft g

Blends

Directions: Say the name of each picture. Print its beginning blend on the line. Trace the rest of the word.

RULE

A **consonant blend** is two or more consonants that come together in a word. Their sounds blend together, but each sound is heard.

1. _____ ag

2. _____ ail

3. _____ og

4. _____ ed

5. _____ ide

6. _____ esent

7. _____ ack

8. _____ ill

9. _____ agon

10. _____ ug

11. _____ ar

12. _____ acker

13. _____ own

14. _____ obe

Blends

Directions: Underline the beginning blend in each word. Then use the words to complete the riddles below.

p l u m	s t a i r s	c r i b
p r i n c e	b l o c k s	s w i n g s
b r i d g e	s n o w	g l a s s

1. You use it to go up and down. What is it? _____

2. It is cold, white, and wet. What is it? _____

3. It is something to eat. What is it? _____

4. A baby sleeps in it. What is it? _____

5. I can drink water from it. What is it? _____

6. Some day he will be king. Who is it? _____

7. You use it to cross a river. What is it? _____

8. You can play on it. What is it? _____

9. You can build with it. What is it? _____

Blends

Directions: Say the name of each picture. Listen carefully for its final blend. Then circle the word.

RULE

A **consonant blend** is two or more consonants that come together in a word. Their sounds blend together, but each sound is heard.

1.

gold   golf
gift   gasp

2.

pest   ants
pants   pink

3.

gent   went
gift   bent

4.

cast   camp
candy   lamp

5.

toast   most
post   coast

6.

milk   sift
silk   sink

7.

best   bank
blank   rand

8.

sad   hand
sand   stand

9.

pest   west
wink   nest

10.

swing   string
sting   sling

11.

mast   milk
melt   belt

12.

fist   fling
fast   film

13.

raft   left
lest   deft

14.

gymnast   gym
wrist   quest

Blends

Directions: Unscramble the word to complete the sentence. Print it on the line. (*Hint:* The letters for the blend in each word are already together.)

1. The _____ grabbed the nut.	r r i s q u e l
2. I am afraid of _____ .	k a s n e s
3. I see a flag flying at the _____ .	n k a b
4. The _____ and groom will go to the coast.	e d i b r
5. The _____ is green on my block.	g r s a s
6. We stepped on the _____ .	p a t r
7. We have _____ on the playground.	i n g s s w
8. I _____ when I eat strawberries!	e l i s m
9. That gymnast has the most _____ ribbons.	e u b l
10. Her _____ likes to sing.	s s a c l
11. She got her _____ for a great price!	s s e d r
12. He plays the _____ in the band.	m u d r

y as a Vowel

Directions: Use the words to solve the riddles.

> ## RULE
> Sometimes **y** can stand for the vowel sound of long **e** as in the word *happy*.

tiny	funny	hurry	sleepy	happy

1. tired and ready for bed _____

2. it makes me laugh _____

3. not sad _____

4. very, very small _____

5. go fast _____

> ## RULE
> When **y** is the only vowel at the end of a one-syllable word, it usually has the long **i** sound as in *cry*.

why	my	by	try	sly

6. sneaky _____

7. it's a question _____

8. do your best _____

9. next to something _____

10. belongs to me _____

y as a Vowel

Directions: Read the words. Decide if the **y** makes the sound of long **e** or long **i**. In every box, connect the two words with the long **e** sound and connect the two words with the long **i** sound.

1.		**2.**	
mommy	thy	frilly	dizzy
why	fuzzy	ply	try
3.		**4.**	
Ky	sky	by	Sally
daddy	marry	dairy	pry

Directions: Name each picture. If the **y** make the long **e** sound, circle *long e*. If the **y** make the long **i** sound, circle *long i*.

5. long e long i	**6.** long e long i	**7.** long e long i	**8.** long e long i
berry	sky	fly	fairy
9. long e long i	**10.** long e long i	**11.** long e long i	**12.** long e long i
fry	candy	dry	penny

Consonant Digraphs

Directions: Read each sentence. Circle the words that have the consonant digraphs **sh**, **ch**, **th**, **wh**, or **ck**. Then, write *yes* if the sentence is true and *no* if it is not true.

> **RULE**
>
> A **consonant digraph** is two consonants that make one sound. You can hear consonant digraphs in *shop, chip, that, who,* and *pick.*

1. I have two thumbs. _____

2. Shells grow in gardens. _____

3. A cherry is a small fruit. _____

4. A person can think. _____

5. Shoes go on feet. _____

6. A duck says moo. _____

7. I can sit on a chair. _____

8. You can drink a whistle. _____

9. A candle has a wick. _____

10. A shuttle can fly in space. _____

11. A whale can swim. _____

12. A baby has 100 teeth. _____

13. A ship can float. _____

Consonant Digraphs

Directions: Complete each sentence with a word with the consonant digraph **kn**. Print the word on the line.

RULE

The **consonant digraph kn** makes the sound of **n** as in *knit*.

---

1. I bumped my _____.

know
knee

---

2. I am learning to _____.

knit
knob

---

3. The _____ is guarding the castle.

knew
knight

---

4. She cut the bread with a _____.

knight
knife

---

5. I _____ the answer.

knot
know

---

6. Turn the _____ and go inside.

knob
know

---

7. Ring the bell or _____ on the door.

knob
knock

---

8. I _____ her before this class.

knew
knot

---

9. You will need to _____ to pull the weeds.

knight
kneel

Consonant Digraphs

Directions: Read the words in the first column that describe the item. Then read the second column to find the rhyming word. Print the answer in the third column.

> **RULE**
> The **consonant digraph wr** makes the sound **r** as in *wrap*.

wrinkle   wriggle   wrench   wrestle   wren   write

wreck   wrist   wrap   wrong   wreath

a tool	rhymes with bench	1. _____
Christmas decoration	rhymes with teeth	2. _____
an accident	rhymes with deck	3. _____
a bird	rhymes with pen	4. _____
not right	rhymes with song	5. _____
struggle with someone or something	rhymes with vessel	6. _____
to cover	rhymes with tap	7. _____
body part	rhymes with fist	8. _____
put letters on paper	rhymes with bite	9. _____
to move back and forth	rhymes with giggle	10. _____
folds or creases on skin or cloth	rhymes with twinkle	11. _____

Consonant Digraphs

Directions: Say the name of each picture. Circle the consonant digraph that you hear.

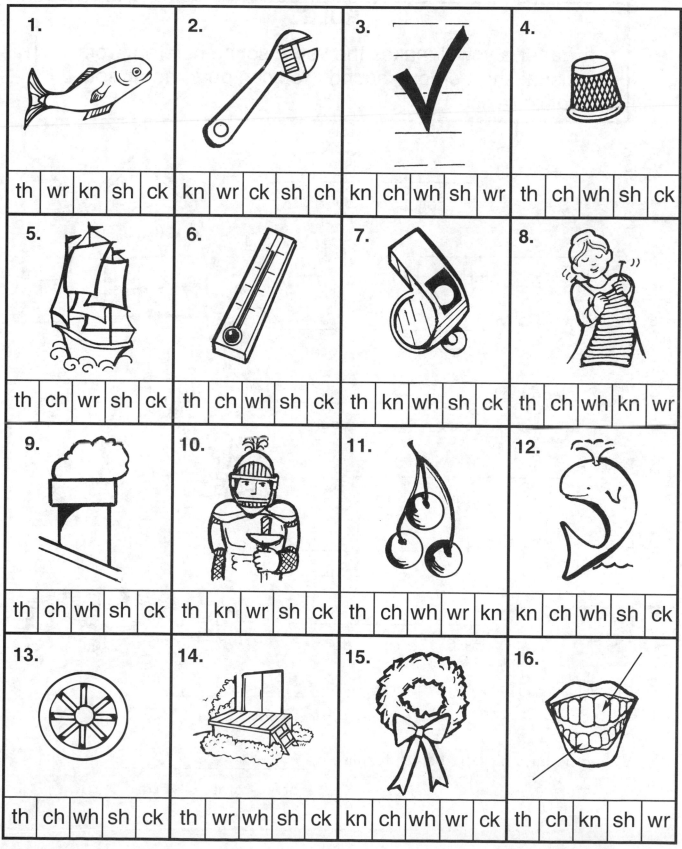

1. th | wr | kn | sh | ck
2. kn | wr | ck | sh | ch
3. kn | ch | wh | sh | wr
4. th | ch | wh | sh | ck

5. th | ch | wr | sh | ck
6. th | ch | wh | sh | ck
7. th | kn | wh | sh | ck
8. th | ch | wh | kn | wr

9. th | ch | wh | sh | ck
10. th | kn | wr | sh | ck
11. th | ch | wh | wr | kn
12. kn | ch | wh | sh | ck

13. th | ch | wh | sh | ck
14. th | wr | wh | sh | ck
15. kn | ch | wh | wr | ck
16. th | ch | kn | sh | wr

r-Controlled Vowels

Directions: Complete each sentence with an **r**-controlled word. Print the word on the line.

RULE

An **r** after a vowel makes the vowel sound different from the usual short or long sound. You can hear the **ar** sound in *star* or *park*.

---

1. Bart wants to get a _____ .

far   car   tar

2. He will _____ a part-time job.

star   stark   start

3. He will work on a _____ .

farm   far   harm

4. He will clean the _____ .

bard   bart   barn

5. It will be _____ .

harp   hard   hart

6. Bart will need strong _____ .

harms   farms   arms

7. He will work until _____ .

dark   dart   darn

8. He will save his money in a large _____ .

far   bark   jar

9. When he buys his car, he will feel like a _____ !

garb   star   yarn

R-Controlled Vowels

Directions: Read the sentences. Find the matching picture. Put the number of the sentence in the box next to the picture.

RULE

An **r** after a vowel makes the vowel sound different from the usual short or long sound. You can hear the **or** sound in *horn* and *fork*.

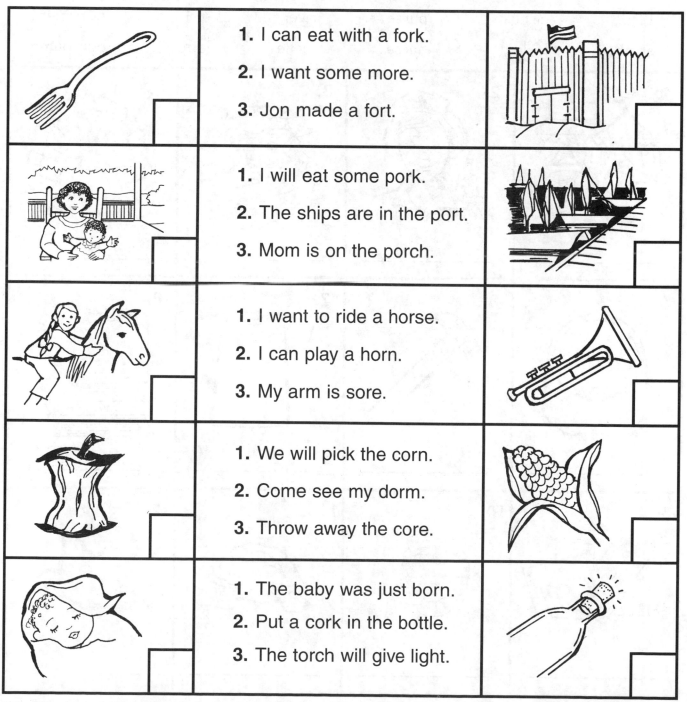

1. I can eat with a fork.
2. I want some more.
3. Jon made a fort.

1. I will eat some pork.
2. The ships are in the port.
3. Mom is on the porch.

1. I want to ride a horse.
2. I can play a horn.
3. My arm is sore.

1. We will pick the corn.
2. Come see my dorm.
3. Throw away the core.

1. The baby was just born.
2. Put a cork in the bottle.
3. The torch will give light.

r-Controlled Vowels

Directions: Say the name of each picture. Print its name under it. Use the list of words to help you.

RULE

An **r** after a vowel makes the vowel sound different from the usual short or long sound. You can hear the **ir** sound in *fir*, the **er** sound in *fern*, and the **ur** sound in *fur*.

| bird | circus | purse | river | girl | hammer |
| shirt | turkey | nurse | turtle | letters | computer |

r-Controlled Vowels

Directions: Read each word. Look at the vowel followed by the letter **r**. Print the word in the correct box.

ar   **or**

sir	card
purr	verse
form	over
dart	chirp
first	turn
storm	far
burst	fir
store	perk
torch	fur
burn	sort
her	serve
dirt	bark

ar	or
dart	

ir   **er**   **ur**

ir	er	ur

Unit Review

Directions: Say the name of each picture. Circle the correct word.

1.	2.	3.	4.
giggle goggle coddle gobble	silly Sunday sunny Sally	dress drum drag dragon	click clack clock cluck

5.	6.	7.	8.
garbage grip garden guard	my fry shy dry	birdcage barnyard	thick thimble tumble thumb

9.	10.	11.	12.
nice rice ice dice	flagpole flashlight	pork port perch porch	wrist wrap wring wrong

13.	14.	15.	16.
twigs twist twill twins	brash brush brick rush	firm form farm far	batter bitter butter better

Unit Review

Directions: Find the word that will complete the sentence. Print it on the line.

| castle | dragon | fork | white | ice cream | Sally |
| shy | giant | lunch | letter | mailbox | table |

1. I know a story about a _____ princess.

2. Her name is _____ .

3. She lives in a huge _____ .

4. Six days ago, she wrote a _____ .

5. She put it in the _____ .

6. She sent it to a _____ dragon.

7. She made a nice, _____ cake.

8. The dragon came to _____ .

9. Sally set the _____ .

10. They each got a knife, a spoon, and a _____ .

11. She served the cake and _____ .

12. Sally and the giant _____ were happy!

UNIT 5
Contractions, Endings, and Suffixes

Contractions

Contractions are a short way of writing two words. It is formed by putting two words together and leaving out one or more letters. An apostrophe is used to show where something is left out. Some contractions are formed with the words *not*, *is*, and *have*. Such contractions are *can't*, *he's*, and *I've*.

Directions: Print the <u>two words</u> that mean the same as the underlined word in each sentence.

1. <u>Don't</u> wait to go sledding!	_____ _____
2. <u>It's</u> hard to wait for the snow.	_____ _____
3. <u>We've</u> got a brand new sled.	_____ _____
4. I <u>haven't</u> used it yet.	_____ _____
5. I <u>won't</u> if it does not snow.	_____ _____

Directions: Print the <u>contraction</u> that means the same as the two words beside the line.

6. are not = _____	**11.** do not = _____
7. did not = _____	**12.** will not = _____
8. he is = _____	**13.** she is = _____
9. that is = _____	**14.** I have = _____
10. we have = _____	**15.** they have = _____

Contractions

Some contractions are formed with the words *am*, *are*, *will*, and *us*. Such contractions are *I'm*, *we're*, and *let's*.

Directions: Print the <u>two words</u> that mean the same as the underlined word in each sentence.

1. <u>I'm</u> going to the store tomorrow.	_____ _____
2. <u>We're</u> going to have a party today.	_____ _____
3. <u>Let's</u> buy a special cake.	_____ _____
4. <u>I'll</u> buy the decorations.	_____ _____
5. <u>He'll</u> bring the ice cream.	_____ _____

Directions: Print the <u>contraction</u> that means the same as the two words beside the line.

6. we will = _____	**11.** he will = _____
7. I am = _____	**12.** you are = _____
8. we are = _____	**13.** I will = _____
9. let us = _____	**14.** they are = _____
10. they will = _____	**15.** she will = _____

Contractions Review

Directions: Read the sentences below. Find the contraction that has the same meaning as the two words that are underlined. Fill in the bubble beside the correct answer.

1. <u>We will</u> go skiing this winter.	◯ We'll ◯ Won't ◯ We've
2. Tom <u>does not</u> have skis.	◯ didn't ◯ doesn't ◯ don't
3. <u>He will</u> skate instead.	◯ Hill ◯ He'll ◯ I'll
4. He thinks <u>it is</u> more fun.	◯ I's ◯ he's ◯ it's
5. <u>We have</u> a brand new sled.	◯ We're ◯ Won't ◯ We've
6. <u>I am</u> going to ride it first.	◯ I'm ◯ I'll ◯ I'am
7. Sue <u>will not</u> want to ride.	◯ we're ◯ won't ◯ we've
8. <u>She will</u> ski instead.	◯ Shed ◯ She'll ◯ She'd
9. Sue thinks <u>we are</u> silly.	◯ we're ◯ won't ◯ we've
10. <u>I am</u> happy to ski and to sled.	◯ Iam ◯ I'm ◯ it's
11. <u>They will</u> both make me happy.	◯ They'll ◯ The ◯ They've
12. <u>It is</u> fun to play in the winter.	◯ Its ◯ I'm ◯ It's

Contractions Review

Directions: Read the sentences below. Circle the contraction that best completes the sentence.

1. The children shouted, "(**Its, It's**) snowing."

2. "(**Who's, Whose**) ready to play outside?" Sue asked.

3. "(**I'll, I'm**) ready," said Sam.

4. "(**I'll, It'll**) get my sled," Tom said.

5. "I know (**we'll, well**) have fun in the snow today," said Mary.

6. Joe said that (**he'll, his**) bring along his skates.

7. Jane said that (**she'll, shell**) bring along her skis.

8. "(**They'd, That's**) better hurry up!" said Sue.

9. "(**Lets, Let's**) go!" shouted Sam.

10. "(**Were, We're**) off!" they all shouted.

Plural Endings

RULE

When **s** or **es** is added to a word, it forms the plural. Plural means more than one. If a word ends in **x**, **z**, **ss**, **sh**, or **ch**, usually add **es** to make it mean more than one, such as *wash = washes* or *church = churches*. For other words, just add **s**, such as lap = laps.

Directions: Read the sentences below. Circle the word that will finish each sentence. Print it on the line.

1. We are going to see the _____ at the zoo. animal animals	
2. First, we will go see the three _____ . elephant elephants	
3. Next, I will run to see the three baby _____ . foxs foxes	
4. Then, I will go to see the two _____ . hippopotamus hippopotamuses	
5. I will then have a break and eat some _____ . peach peaches	

Plural Endings

Directions: Read the packing list below. Finish each word by adding the ending **s** or **es**. Print the ending on the line.

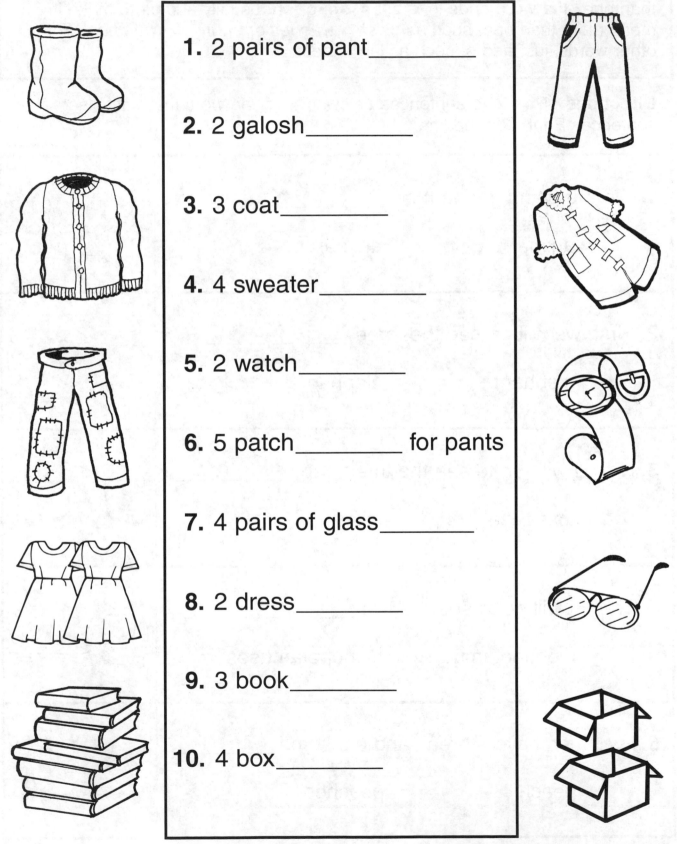

1. 2 pairs of pant_____

2. 2 galosh_____

3. 3 coat_____

4. 4 sweater_____

5. 2 watch_____

6. 5 patch_____ for pants

7. 4 pairs of glass_____

8. 2 dress_____

9. 3 book_____

10. 4 box_____

Inflectional Endings

RULE

Base words are words that can be changed into new words by adding **ing** or **ed**. Some examples include the following:

boat + ing = boating   turn + ed = turned

Directions: Read the sentences below. Adding **ing** or **ed** to the word beside each sentence. Print the new word on the line.

1. We _____ to the zoo today.	walk
2. It was _____ so I wore a raincoat.	rain
3. The monkeys were _____ trees.	climb
4. They _____ in the rain.	play
5. The kangaroos were _____ .	jump
6. They didn't like _____ wet.	be
7. The sun was _____ to shine.	start
8. The animals were soon _____ .	sleep

Inflectional Endings

RULE

When a short vowel word ends in a single consonant, the consonant is usually doubled before adding the **ing**.

Examples: hop + ing = hopping   jog + ing = jogging

Directions: Adding **ing** to the base word in each sentence. Print the new word on the line.

1. Yesterday I went _____ in the pool.
swim

2. I went _____ at the mall.
shop

3. Clean your hands by _____ them together with soap.
rub

4. He began _____ at me.
grin

5. The car was _____ for the children.
stop

6. The horse was _____ in the field.
trot

7. The cow was _____ to the barn.
run

8. The bunny was _____ in the field.
hop

Inflectional Endings

RULE
To make a word tell about the past, **ed** is usually added. If a short vowel word ends in a single consonant, the consonant is usually doubled before adding **ed**.
Examples: hop + ed = hopped   jog + ed = jogged

Directions: Add **ed** to each base word. Print the new word on the line.

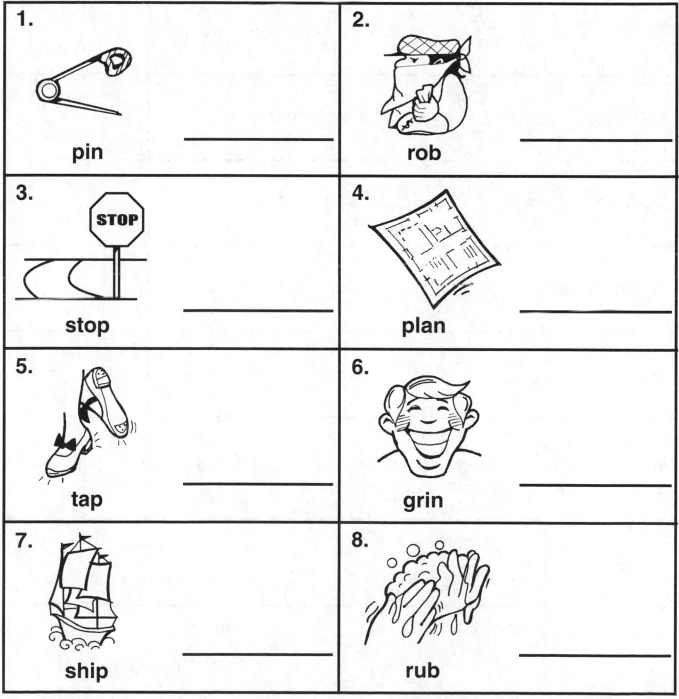

1.

pin _____

2.

rob _____

3.

stop _____

4.

plan _____

5.

tap _____

6.

grin _____

7.

ship _____

8.

rub _____

Inflectional Endings

RULE

If a word ends with a silent **e**, drop the **e** before adding **ing** or **ed**.
Examples: skate + ed = skated   save + ing = saving

Directions: Read the sentences below. Circle the word that completes each sentence and print it on the line.

1. Dad _____ for the president.	voted voting
2. I was _____ a cake for the party.	baked baking
3. Sister _____ a piece for me.	sliced slicing
4. Brother was _____ the rocket.	fired firing
5. Mom _____ the carrots.	diced dicing

Directions: Read each pair of sentences below. Add **ed** or **ing** to the base word and print it on the line to complete each sentence.

save	**6.** My family is _____ for a vacation. Sue's family has _____ for their trip.
ice	**7.** My dad is _____ his cake. My mom already _____ her cake.

110

Inflectional Endings Review

Directions: Read the words below. Add **ing** to each base word. Print the new word on the line.

1. pin _____

2. save _____

3. clean _____

4. skip _____

5. wave _____

6. walk _____

7. stomp _____

8. poke _____

9. swing _____

10. ride _____

11. hop _____

12. hope _____

Directions: Add **ed** to the word beside each sentence to make it tell about the past. Print the word on the line.

13. Yesterday I _____ to the park.	skip
14. I _____ to school.	walk
15. I _____ to the party.	skate
16. He _____ with me on the playground.	play
17. I _____ the tail on the donkey.	pin

Inflectional Endings Review

Directions: Use some of the words in the box below to tell about Susie's party. After writing about the event, illustrate your story.

walked	wished	hoping	swimming
liked	making	wrapped	coming
writing	asking	asked	driving

_____

- -

_____

- -

_____

- -

_____

- -

_____

- -

My Illustration

Suffixes (-ful, -ly)

RULE
You can add endings to words to make new words.
Examples: use + ful = useful   slow + ly = slowly

Directions: Add the ending **ful** or **ly** to each word below. Print the new word on the line.

1. play_____

2. help_____

3. hope_____

4. quick_____

Directions: Use the new words above to complete each sentence below.

5. Tom was _____ he would get a new puppy.

6. He hoped the dog would be very _____ .

7. He has been very _____ to his mother.

8. Tom did his chores _____ .

Directions: Draw a circle around each base word.

9.	s l o w l y	10.	c h e e r f u l
11.	c a r e f u l	12.	u s e f u l
13.	w i s h f u l	14.	l o u d l y
15.	q u i c k l y	16.	b r a v e l y

Suffixes (-less, -ness)

RULE

You can add endings to words to make new words.

Examples: use + less = useless   soft + ness = softness

Directions: Add the ending **less** or **ness** to each word below. Print the new word on each line beside the base word.

1. good _____

2. dark _____

3. home _____

4. moon _____

Diections: Use the new words above to complete each sentence below.

5. It was a _____ night.

6. The _____ was very black.

7. Joe was happy he was not _____.

8. He was glad for the _____ of his own family.

Directions: Draw a picture of your family.

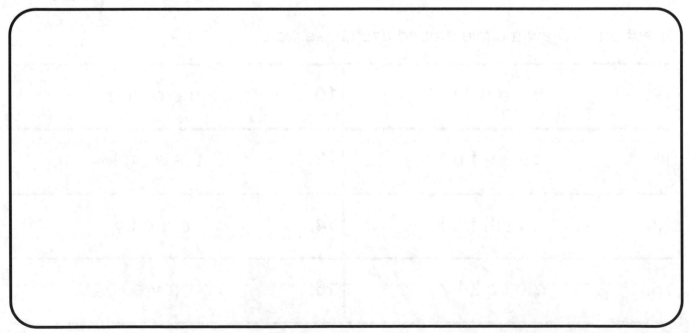

Suffixes Review (-ly, -ful, -less, -ness)

Directions: Read each sentence below. Identify words that have suffixes and circle those words.

1. I love to walk quietly into my bedroom each night.

2. I enjoy the happiness my own room brings me.

3. I love to feel the softness of my pillow.

4. Safe in my covers, it will not be a sleepless night.

5. Knowing I have a safe home makes me joyful.

Directions: Write your own sentences below using words with suffixes. Circle the words that are suffixes.

6. _____

7. _____

8. _____

9. _____

10. _____

More Suffixes (-er, -est)

RULE

You can add an ending to a base word to make a new word that compares things. Add the ending **er** to a word to mean more. Add **est** to a word to signify the most.

Example: long, longer, longest

Directions: Add the ending **er** or **est** to each word below. Print the new words on the lines.

Base Word	More	Most
1. soft	_____	_____
2. great	_____	_____
3. fast	_____	_____
4. short	_____	_____
5. cute	_____	_____
6. strange	_____	_____
7. hard	_____	_____
8. small	_____	_____
9. mad	_____	_____
10. smart	_____	_____

More Suffixes (-er, -est)

RULE

When a word ends in **y** after a consonant, change the **y** to an **i** before adding **er** or **est**.

Example: sunny + est = sunniest

Directions: Add the ending **er** or **est** to each word below. Print the new words on the lines.

1. It will be _____ tomorrow.

rainy

2. January is _____ than July.

chilly

3. August is usually the _____ month.

sunny

4. Sometimes it is _____ in March.

windy

5. The clouds are _____ in the summer.

fluffy

6. The roads are _____ in the winter.

snowy

More Suffixes (-es)

Directions: Change the **y** to **i** and add **es** to each word below. Print the words on the lines.

1. bunny	2. cherry	3. daisy
_____	_____	_____
4. city	5. party	6. penny
_____	_____	_____
7. candy	8. pony	9. lily
_____	_____	_____
10. puppy	11. story	12. family
_____	_____	_____
13. strawberry	14. baby	15. dairy
_____	_____	_____

Contractions, Endings, and Suffixes Review

Directions: Print each word from the list below in the correct box. Print two contractions in the last box.

darkness	coming	helpful	lowly	cloudier
rested	making	happiness	patches	brushes
silliest	jumped	quickly	careful	smarter

ed	ing	ly

ful	es	ness

er	est	**Print two contractions.**
		_____ _____

Contractions, Endings, and Suffixes Review

Directions: Add the ending from the box to finish the word in each sentence. Print the ending on the line and then trace the whole word.

1. Jenny wish_____ she had a magic wand.	ed
2. If she did, she could make fox_____ sing.	es
3. She would enjoy a sing_____ fox!	ing
4. A magic wand would be very use_____ .	ful
5. Jenny could become the smart_____ girl in school.	est
6. She could have love_____ dress_____ .	ly es
7. Her shoes would be cool_____ than all others.	er
8. Sudden_____ Jenny was glad she did_____ have a wand.	ly n't
9. Tommy is the great_____ tennis player in the world.	est

Contractions, Endings, and Suffixes Review

Directions: It is snowing! Write a story about a snowy day using some of the words from the box below. Then illustrate your story.

skiing	snowing	it's	snowed	happier
skating	faster	we'll	careful	useless
drifted	misses	looked	floated	wishing
quickly	darkness	cheerful	thickest	happiest

My Illustration

Unit Review

Directions: Fill in the bubble beside the word that names or describes each picture.

1.
○ fox
○ boxes
○ foxes

2.
○ bake
○ barker
○ baker

3.
○ dishes
○ ditches
○ dish

4.
○ reading
○ ready
○ red

5.
○ teach
○ teacher
○ toucher

AaBbC

6.
○ cherry
○ chairs
○ cherries

7.
○ patches
○ peaches
○ peach

8.
○ sung
○ singing
○ sink

9.
○ tall
○ taller
○ tailing

10.
○ play
○ playing
○ planing

11.
○ robbing
○ rubbing
○ rubbed

12.
○ running
○ run
○ raining

Unit Reveiw

Directions: Find the word in the box that will complete each sentence. Print the word on the line.

darkness	happily	jumped	swished
sledding	scariest	watched	couldn't
hardly	softly		

1. The snow fell _____ on the hill.

2. I _____ the flakes fall from my window.

3. Tomorrow I'll be _____ !

4. I could _____ wait for morning.

5. Soon the _____ left, and it was morning.

6. I _____ grabbed my sled and raced to the hill.

7. First, I _____ onto my sleigh.

8. Then I was on the _____ ride of all.

9. The sleigh _____ down the hill.

10. Safe at the bottom, I _____ wait to go again.

UNIT 6
Vowel Pairs, Digraphs, and Diphthongs

Vowel Pairs (ai, ay)

Directions: Say the name of each picture. Circle its name.

RULE

In a **vowel pair**, two vowels come together to make one long vowel sound. The first vowel stands for the long sound and the second vowel is silent. You can hear the long **a** sound in *sail* and *pay*.

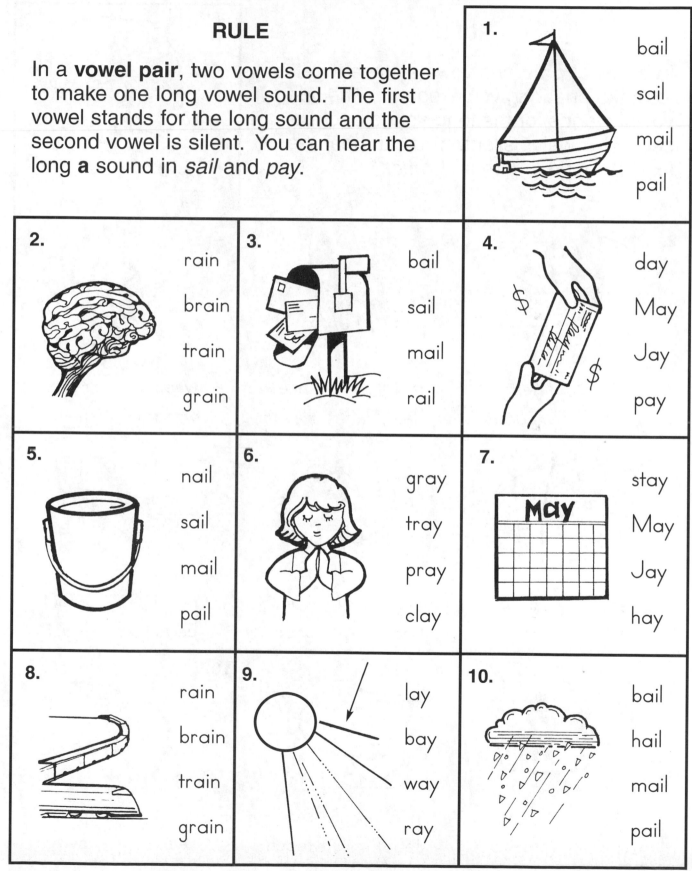

1.
- bail
- sail
- mail
- pail

2.
- rain
- brain
- train
- grain

3.
- bail
- sail
- mail
- rail

4.
- day
- May
- Jay
- pay

5.
- nail
- sail
- mail
- pail

6.
- gray
- tray
- pray
- clay

7.
- stay
- May
- Jay
- hay

8.
- rain
- brain
- train
- grain

9.
- lay
- bay
- way
- ray

10.
- bail
- hail
- mail
- pail

Vowel Pairs (ee, ea)

Directions: Say the name of each picture. Circle its name.

RULE

In a **vowel pair**, two vowels come together to make one long vowel sound. The first vowel stands for the long sound and the second vowel is silent. You can hear the long **e** sound in *bee* and *meat*.

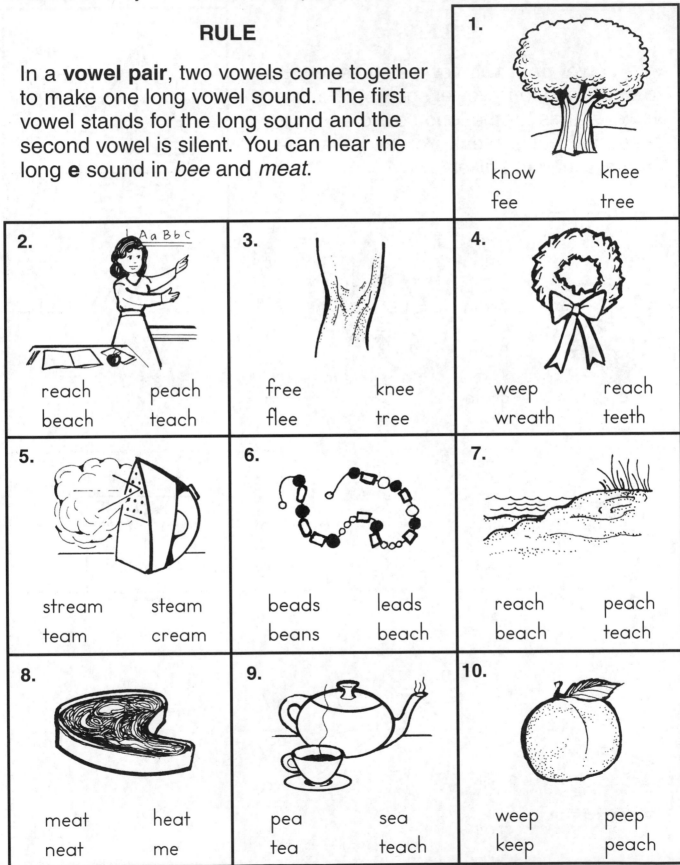

1.

know   knee

fee   tree

2.

reach   peach

beach   teach

3.

free   knee

flee   tree

4.

weep   reach

wreath   teeth

5.

stream   steam

team   cream

6.

beads   leads

beans   beach

7.

reach   peach

beach   teach

8.

meat   heat

neat   me

9.

pea   sea

tea   teach

10.

weep   peep

keep   peach

Vowel Pairs (ie, oe)

Directions: Read each sentence. Fill in the bubble beside the sentence that tells about the picture.

RULE

In a **vowel pair**, two vowels come together to make one long vowel sound. The first vowel stands for the long sound and the second vowel is silent. You can hear the long **i** sound in *lie* and the long **o** sound in *toe*.

1.	○ I cannot tell a lie. ○ The cat is telling a lie. ○ The cat will lie down.
2.	○ Your plant wants a piece of pie. ○ Water your plant or it will die. ○ Your plant is going to die.
3.	○ She will talk to Joe in the garden. ○ Her hoe is broken. ○ She will use her hoe in the garden.
4.	○ My dog is named Joe. ○ My sister is named Joe. ○ My brother is named Joe.
5.	○ We made an apple pie. ○ I want to eat an apple. ○ The dog ran off with the pie.

Vowel Pairs (ow, oa)

Directions: Say the name of each picture. Print its name under it. Use the words in the box to help you.

RULE

In a **vowel pair**, two vowels come together to make one long vowel sound. The vowel pair **ow** sometimes has the long **o** sound as in *snow*. The vowel pair **oa** has the long **o** sound as in *goat*.

coat

mow

crow

moat

float

bowl

blow

rowboat

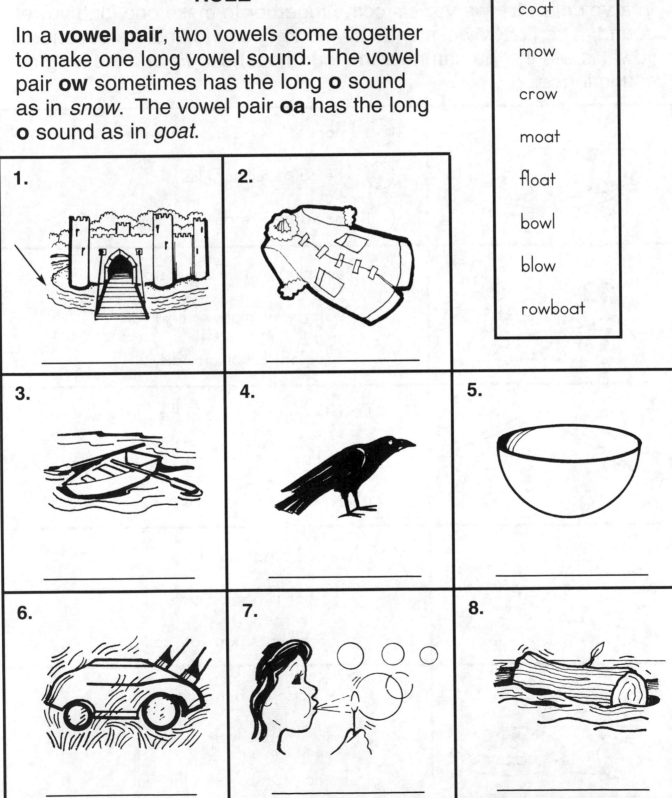

1. _____

2. _____

3. _____

4. _____

5. _____

6. _____

7. _____

8. _____

Vowel Pairs

Directions: Connect the dots to make a picture. Begin at the top star and connect all of the vowel pairs with the **long a** or **long e** sound. Next, begin at the bottom star. Connect all of the vowel pairs with the **long o** or **long i** sound.

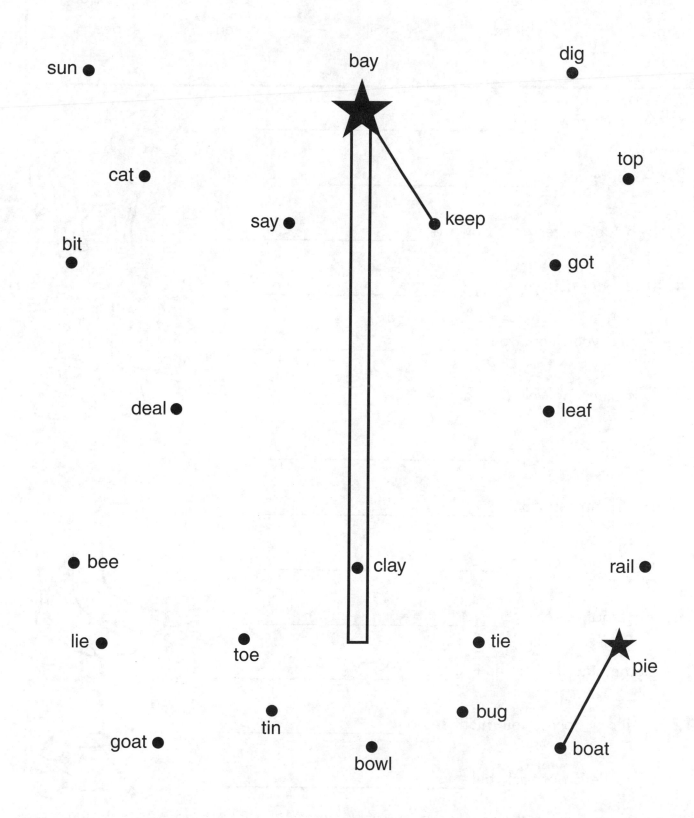

Vowel Pairs

Directions: Read each word in the box. Circle its vowel pair. Use each word to complete the riddle. Print the answers on the line.

drain	feel	slow	boat	rainbow
toes	bleed	tail	green	neat
doe	dream	hay		

1. A dog can wag its _____ .

2. A horse eats _____ .

3. In a tub, water goes down a _____ .

4. If you get cut, you will _____ .

5. When you sleep, you _____ .

6. Mix blue and yellow to get _____ .

7. Use your fingers to _____ .

8. It is not messy, but _____ .

9. Each foot has five _____ .

10. A female deer is a _____ .

11. Something that floats is a _____ .

12. After a storm, you might see a _____ .

13. A turtle is not fast, but _____ .

Vowel Digraphs (oo)

RULE

In a **vowel digraph**, two vowels together can make a long or a short sound, or have a special sound all their own. You can hear the different sounds of the vowel digraph **oo** in *zoo* or in *book*.

Directions: Name the picture. Circle its name.

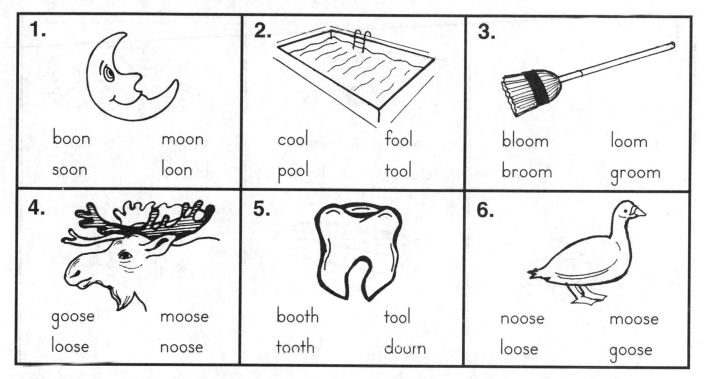

1.	**2.**	**3.**
boon moon soon loon	cool fool pool tool	bloom loom broom groom
4.	**5.**	**6.**
goose moose loose noose	booth tool tooth doom	noose moose loose goose

Directions: Print the name of the sound on the line next to the item that makes it.

7. A race car goes _____ .

8. A cannon goes _____ .

9. A ghost goes _____ .

10. A cow goes _____ .

11. A baby goes _____ .

12. A dove goes _____ .

13. A little sister says, "Me, _____ !"

14. A person with a cold says, "_____ !"

boom
moo
too
coo
boo
goo
Achoo
varoom

Vowel Digraphs (oo)

RULE

In a **vowel digraph**, two vowels together can make a long or a short sound, or have a special sound all their own. You can hear the different sounds of the vowel digraph **oo** in *zoo* or in *book*.

Directions: Name the picture. Circle its name.

1.		2.		3.	
rook	nook	hood	wood	book	rook
cook	book	stood	hook	brook	crook

4.		5.		6.	
crook	cook	good	wood	brook	hook
look	rook	hood	stood	hood	took

Directions: Follow the directions to change the word *good* into the word *rook*.

7. Begin with good.

good

8. Change g to w.

9. Change w to h.

10. Change d to k.

11. Change h to t.

12. Change t to l.

13. Change l to n.

14. Change n to r.

Vowel Digraphs (ea)

RULE

In a **vowel digraph**, two vowels together can make a long or a short sound, or have a special sound all their own. You can hear the short **e** sound of the vowel digraph **ea** in *head*.

Directions: Read the sentences. Find the matching picture. Put the number of the sentence in the box next to the picture.

	1. He has a cap on his head. **2.** I am going swimming. **3.** I think my plant is dead.	
	1. I read this book already. **2.** The pencil's lead is sharp. **3.** I ate some bread.	
	1. Walk with a soft tread. **2.** I need to use the thread. **3.** I just made some bread.	
	1. I need to wear a sweater. **2.** It is made of leather. **3.** I found a bird's feather.	
	1. I need to take a breath. **2.** Let's eat breakfast. **3.** Today's weather is sunny.	

Vowel Digraphs (au, aw)

RULE

In a **vowel digraph**, two vowels together can make a long or a short sound, or have a special sound all their own. You can hear the sound of **au** and **aw** in *haul* and *saw*.

Directions: Read the clues. Find the word in the box. Write the word in the crossword puzzle.

crawl	raw
paw	saw
draw	Paul
haul	dawn
laws	lawn
straw	

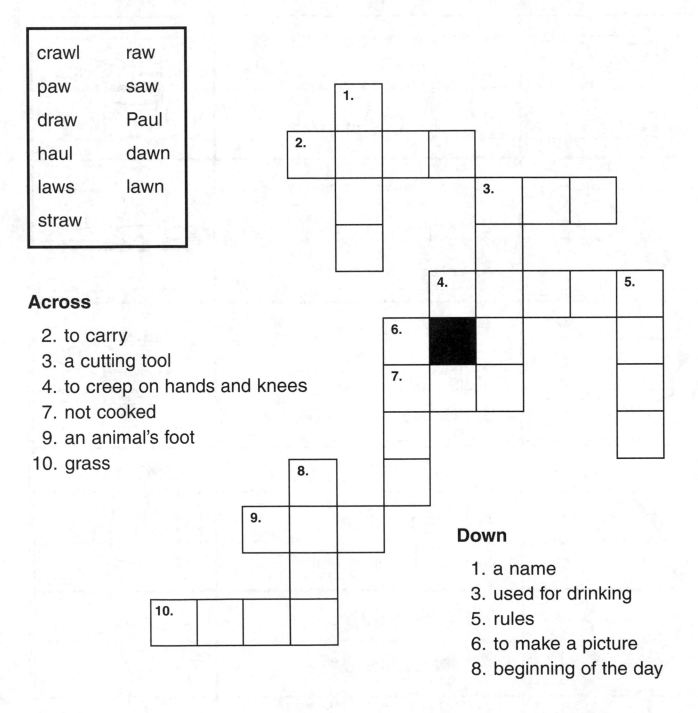

Across

2. to carry
3. a cutting tool
4. to creep on hands and knees
7. not cooked
9. an animal's foot
10. grass

Down

1. a name
3. used for drinking
5. rules
6. to make a picture
8. beginning of the day

Vowel Digraphs

Directions: Read the words in the first column that describes the item. Look in the second column for a rhyming word. Print the answer in the third column.

ready   hawk   good   bawl   brook

bread   loose   cool   fawn   cookie

pause   groom   Heather

a baby deer	rhymes with pawn	1. _____
food	rhymes with tread	2. _____
a sweet treat	rhymes with rookie	3. _____
not bad	rhymes with wood	4. _____
a bird	rhymes with gawk	5. _____
not hot	rhymes with fool	6. _____
stop for a short time	rhymes with cause	7. _____
all set	rhymes with steady	8. _____
a small river	rhymes with crook	9. _____
not tight	rhymes with noose	10. _____
to cry	rhymes with maul	11. _____
man who marries	rhymes with room	12. _____
a girl's name	rhymes with leather	13. _____

Vowel Digraphs

Directions: Read the directions below and follow them.

1. Color the broom green.

2. Color the stool yellow.

3. Color the sweater red.

4. Color the hawk brown.

5. Color the thread blue.

6. Circle the month of August.

7. Put an X on the books.

8. Underline the hood.

9. Put a check on the straw.

Diphthongs (ou, ow)

RULE

A **diphthong** is made up of two letters blended together to make one sound. You can hear the sound of the diphthongs **ou** and **ow** in *cloud* and *crown*.

Directions: Draw a line from the word to its matching picture.

mouse

cloud

cow

flower

shower

cowboy

hound

house

clown

owl

mouth

towel

crown

round

south

blouse

Diphthongs (ow)

RULE

The letters **ow** can be a vowel pair and stand for the long **o** sound as in *snow*. In other words, the letters **ow** work as a diphthong, making a new sound as in *clown*.

Directions: Help the clown get to the circus. Draw a line from the clown to a word with the diphthong **ow** as in *clown*. Go to the next word with the diphthong **ow** until you reach the town. (*Hint:* Do not draw a line to words if **ow** makes the long **o** sound.)

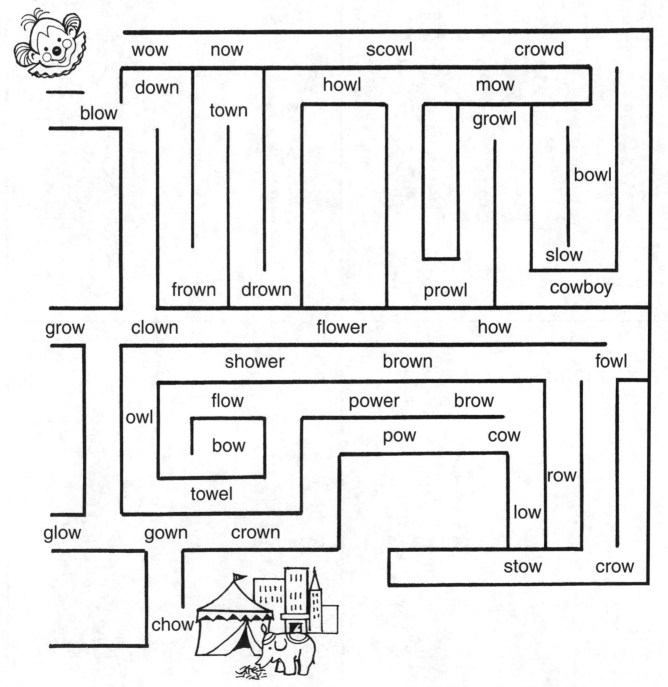

Diphthongs (ow, ou)

Directions: Complete each sentence with a word from the box.

crowds	plow	house	showers	brow	mound
trowel	ground	cloud	flowers	proud	town

I have a garden by my _____ .

Before I plant _____ in it, I will make a plan.

My Plan

1. Go to _____ to buy seeds.

2. Borrow a _____ .

3. Use the plow to prepare the _____ .

4. Dig a small hole with a _____ .

5. Put a seed in the hole and pat a _____ of dirt over it.

6. Wish for a _____ to give me some shade.

7. Wipe my _____ . This is hard work!

8. Wait for rain _____ .

When my flowers grow, I think _____ will come see them!

I will be _____ of my garden.

Diphthongs (oi, oy)

Directions: Read each word. Write the letter of its meaning on the line next to it.

1. coin _____   **a.** cooking liquid

2. toys _____   **b.** very happy

3. oil _____   **c.** money

4. joy _____   **d.** dolls and trucks

5. soil _____   **e.** a name

6. join _____   **f.** bubbling water

7. boil _____   **g.** put together

8. Boyd _____   **h.** dirt

9. boy _____   **i.** way to cook

10. noise _____   **j.** not a girl

11. spoil _____   **k.** loud sound

12. broil _____   **l.** turns bad

Diphthongs (oi, oy)

Directions: Find a row with three words with the **oi** or **oy** diphthong. Draw a line through the three words. On the line, write if the diphthong is **oi** or **oy**.

coil	cow	yawn
head	poise	play
oil	snow	joint

_____

draw	coy	point
toil	Floyd	show
boat	soy	how

_____

Roy	know	choice
paws	poise	now
foil	enjoy	pie

_____

Diphthongs (oi, oy)

Directions: Circle the word in the parentheses that will complete the sentence.

1. Meet Boyd and (Toy, Boy, Roy).

2. They have two friends, Joyce and (Soy, Coy, Joy).

3. Today the (boys, toys, soys) will fix dinner.

4. They will put their (boys, toys, soys) away.

5. The milk was left out so it is (boiled, coiled, spoiled).

6. The boys do not want to use (soy, coy, boy) milk!

7. They will put their (joins, coins, points) together to buy more milk.

8. Then they will (toil, coil, broil) steaks.

9. They plan to offer a (point, choice, noise) of rice or potatoes.

10. They will (boil, toil, oil) water for the rice.

11. They will wrap the potatoes in (soil, oil, foil) and bake them.

12. Roy and Boyd will make a lot of (poise, noise, joint) as they cook!

13. Joy and (Joyce, Ploy, Foil) want to make the salad.

14. They will mix (toil, oil, foil) and vinegar for the salad.

15. I think the boys and girls will (join, coins, enjoy) their dinner!

Diphthongs (ew)

RULE

A **diphthong** is made up of two letters blended together to make one sound. You can hear the long **u** sound of the diphthong **ew** in *mew*.

Directions: Read each sentence. Circle words that have the diphthong **ew**. Then, write *yes* if the sentence is true and *no* if it is not true.

1. A dog goes mew. _____

2. A baby is new. _____

3. Use a hammer for a screw. _____

4. You can eat stew. _____

5. I can chew gum. _____

6. The news is never true. _____

7. The wind blew in the storm. _____

8. Few means ten or more. _____

9. He grew. Now he is smaller. _____

10. The bird flew. _____

11. The football player threw the ball. _____

12. She knew her friends. _____

13. The cat flew away. _____

Diphthongs (oi, oy, ew, ou)

Directions: Print the word under the correct picture. Then circle the diphthong (**oi**, **oy**, **ew**, **ou**) in each word.

cloud	screw	mew	clown	crown	coins
stew	boy	house	toys	flew	soil

1. _____

2. _____

3. _____

4. _____

5. _____

6. _____

7. _____

8. _____

9. _____

10. _____

11. _____

12. _____

Unit Review

Directions: Name each picture. Find a word that has the same vowel sound and same spelling for that sound as the picture. Write it beside the picture.

feather	boys	die	day	foes	yawn
train	beach	see	bowl	zoo	
moat	took	town	tail	mew	

1.

2.

3.

4.

5.

6.

7.

8.

9.

10.

11.

12.

13.

14.

15.

16.

Unit Review

Directions: Say the name of the picture. Circle the vowel pair, digraph, or diphthong that you hear.

1.	2.	3.	4.
ai oo ow ie au	ea ie ai oy ew	aw oe oa oi ew	oy ow ea ie ay

5.	6.	7.	8.
ai oo aw ie oa	ay ie oo ee oy	ay ie ai ee oe	ay ie ai ee oi

9.	10.	11.	12.
ai ou oe ay ea	ai ie oe ow ea	ew aw oo ay ea	ew ai oe ay ea

13.	14.	15.	16.
oa aw au ay oo	oo aw ie ay ea	ew aw oe ai oa	ew aw oo oy ie

Unit Review

Directions: Find the word that will answer the riddle. Print it in the box.

wood	yawn	food	bowl	brain
Joy	crew	peep	cook	breakfast
point	noon	growl	toes	jaw

1. You use it to think. It's in your head. What is it? _____	**2.** A chick makes this sound. What is it? _____	**3.** I have five on each foot. What are they? _____
4. You eat it to stay alive. What is it? _____	**5.** This person fixes food. Who is it? _____	**6.** It comes from trees and burns. What is it? _____
7. I eat this in the morning. What is it? _____	**8.** A bear makes this sound. What is it? _____	**9.** I eat lunch at 12:00. When is that? _____
10. This happens when you are sleepy. What is it? _____	**11.** It holds your teeth in your mouth. What is it? _____	**12.** You can do this with your finger. What is it? _____
13. This is a name for a group of workers. What is it? _____	**14.** This is a dish for eating soup. What is it? _____	**15.** This is a girl's name. What is it? _____

Unit Review

Directions: Find the word that will complete the sentence. Print it on the line.

grew	house	tie	pause	boy	mow	beach
found	soap	coins	breath	zoo	gray	

1. In my billfold, I have both dollars and _____ .

2. All summer long, the plants in my garden _____ .

3. When we go to the _____ , I will build a sand castle.

4. I love to watch the penguins at the _____ .

5. We moved into a big, white _____ .

6. When you wash your hands, use _____ .

7. How long can you hold your _____ ?

8. When you see a comma in a story, you should _____ .

9. I looked for my lost mittens until they were _____ .

10. My dad got a new suit and _____ .

11. Paul is a nice _____ .

12. I can't go until I _____ the lawn.

13. If you mix white and black, you will get _____ .

UNIT 7

Prefixes, Synonyms, Antonyms, and Homonyms

Prefixes (re-)

Adding the prefix **re** to a base word usually means "to do again."

re + do = redo

Redo your homework!

Directions: Add **re** to the word beside each sentence to make a new word. Print the word on the line to finish the sentence.

1. I will _____ the castle.	build
2. I need to _____ my homework.	do
3. The glass needs to be _____ .	filled
4. I want to _____ the song.	play
5. They need to _____ the movie.	make
6. The battery needs to be _____ .	placed
7. We need to _____ his car.	fuel
8. I need to _____ my work.	check

Prefixes (re-)

Directions: Circle the prefix in each word. Print the base word on the line to make a new word.

1. rebuild	_____
2. rewrap	_____
3. rename	_____
4. redirect	_____
5. replay	_____
6. reuse	_____
7. review	_____
8. remake	_____
9. rewrite	_____
10. recheck	_____

Prefixes (un-)

Adding the prefix **un** to a base word usually means the opposite of the original word.

un + load = unload

Directions: Combine the prefix **un** and a base word to make a new word. Print the new word on the line.

1. un + equal =	_____
2. un + likely =	_____
3. un + forseen =	_____
4. un + necessary =	_____
5. un + popular =	_____
6. un + dress =	_____
7. un + lawful =	_____
8. un + usual =	_____
9. un + seen =	_____
10. un + do =	_____

Prefixes (un-)

Directions: Print the one word that means the same as each pair of words on the line to its side. Write a story in the area below using some of those new words.

not happy _____	not dressed _____
not buttoned _____	not done _____
not locked _____	not tied _____
not buckled _____	not packed _____

_____

- -

_____

- -

_____

_____

- -

_____

- -

_____

- -

_____

- -

_____

Prefix Review (un–, re–)

Directions: The **un** and **re** words below are hiding within the word search. Use your detective skills to circle the hiding words.

unfit	undo	uncover	unsafe
unload	untie	unlock	reclaim
rewrap	regain	repack	
reuse	redo	replay	

```
r  e  c  l  a  i  m  t  y  u
e  u  n  c  o  v  e  r  i  u
g  n  r  o  r  e  u  s  e  n
a  s  e  p  a  u  n  f  i  t
i  a  p  z  r  x  d  u  u  i
n  f  l  r  e  d  o  n  n  e
c  e  a  v  w  b  n  l  l  m
s  d  y  f  r  g  h  o  o  j
k  r  e  p  a  c  k  c  a  l
r  e  r  e  p  r  e  k  d  r
```

Prefix Review (un-, re-)

Directions: Print the one word to finish the sentence that means the same as each pair of words in the parentheses.

Example
not locked = unlocked

Example
wind again = rewind

1. I had to _____ the letter to Sue.
(write again)

2. It is very _____ to sleep on the floor.
(not comfortable)

3. I need to _____ my story.
(tell again)

4. I have to _____ my homework.
(view again)

5. Tom was _____ about doing his homework again.
(not happy)

6. He thought it was _____ to redo it.
(not fair)

7. I had to _____ my suitcase.
(pack again)

8. I will be happy to _____ home.
(turn again)

Prefixes (dis-)

Directions: Combine the prefix **dis** and a base word to make a new word. Print the new word on the line.

> Adding the prefix **dis** to a base word usually means the opposite of the original word.
>
> dis + comfort = discomfort

1. dis + appear =	_____
2. dis + like =	_____
3. dis + grace =	_____
4. dis + close =	_____
5. dis + loyal =	_____
6. dis + obey =	_____
7. dis + agree =	_____
8. dis + cover =	_____
9. dis + trust =	_____
10. dis + taste =	_____

Prefixes (dis-)

Directions: Add the prefix **dis** to each underlined word to make a new word that means the opposite. Print the new word on the line.

1. opposite of <u>agree</u>

2. opposite of <u>believe</u>

3. to change the <u>color</u>

4. not <u>connected</u>

5. opposite of <u>taste</u>

6. opposite of <u>honest</u>

7. opposite of <u>join</u>

8. opposite of <u>obey</u>

9. opposite of <u>trust</u>

Prefixes Review (un-, re-, dis-)

Directions: Add the prefix **un, re,** or **dis** to each base word and then print the new word on the line to finish each sentence.

1. Jenny was _____ at her new school.	easy
2. She was afraid she would be _____ to make new friends.	able
3. Amy and Sue saw that Jenny was _____.	happy
4. They didn't _____ her, and they wanted to be her friend.	like
5. Jenny was _____ how good it was to have friends.	minded

Prefixes Review (un-, re-, dis-)

Directions: Add the prefix **un, re,** or **dis** to each base word in the box below. Then print the new word in the correct column.

un-	dis-	re-

_____ agree   _____ dress   _____ button   _____ color

_____ happy   _____ obey   _____ please   _____ lucky

_____ move   _____ brush   _____ wind   _____ do

_____ gain   _____ trust   _____ kind   _____ tie

_____ approve   _____ loyal   _____ order   _____ move

Synonyms

Directions: Print a word from the box to the side of the word that means the same thing.

sick
huge
small
friend
giggle
garbage

1. large _____

2. ill _____

3. trash _____

4. pal _____

5. laugh _____

6. tiny _____

Directions: Print a word that means the same thing as each word below.

7. skinny _____	**8.** naughty _____
9. easy _____	**10.** snooze _____
11. enjoy _____	**12.** gab _____
13. dislike _____	**14.** glad _____

Synonyms

Directions: Choose the **synonym** from below that has almost the same meaning as the puzzle clue. Print the word in the correct box.

CLUES

1. untruth	**4.** wish	**7.** big
2. male	**5.** short	**8.** horse
3. purchase	**6.** soil	**9.** fast

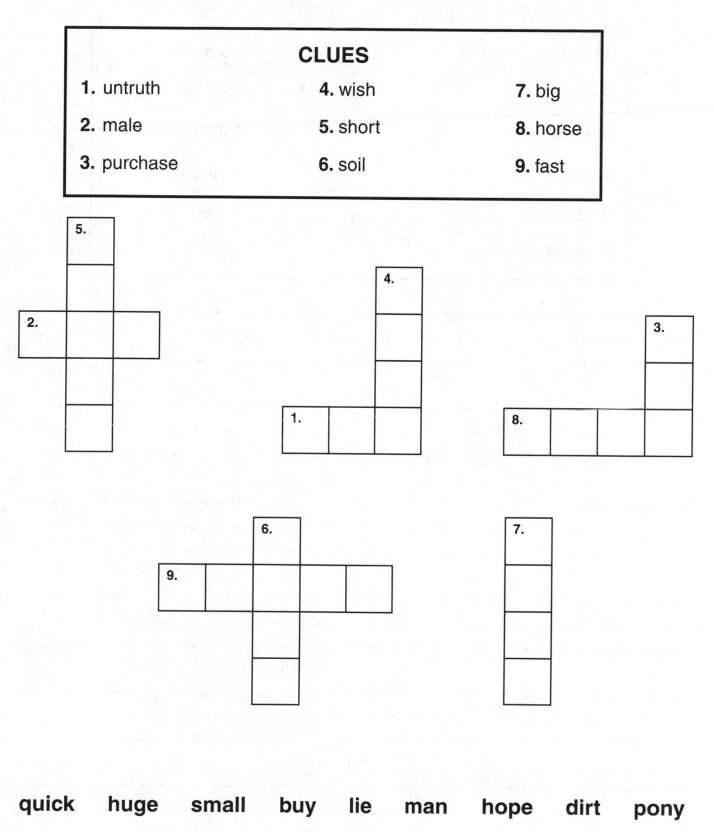

quick   huge   small   buy   lie   man   hope   dirt   pony

Synonyms

Directions: Draw a line to match the words that have the same meaning. Write a story below using some of the **synonyms**.

1. pal	party
2. laugh	happy
3. kind	friend
4. glad	smile
5. grin	nice
6. celebration	giggle

Antonyms

Antonyms are words that are opposite or almost opposite in meaning. *Wet* and *dry* mean the opposite of each other.

Directions: Read each sentence. Circle the letter of the answer that has the opposite meaning from the underlined word in each sentence.

1. Jerry was <u>sad</u> to go into space.

   A. small

   B. happy

   C. sorry

2. He <u>hates</u> to fly in a rocketship.

   A. dislikes

   B. angry

   C. loves

3. First, he will get <u>out of</u> the ship.

   A. inside

   B. around

   C. behind

4. Next, he will <u>pull</u> the door closed.

   A. squeeze

   B. push

   C. punch

5. Then, he will <u>stop</u> the motor.

   A. quit

   B. redep

   C. start

6. The ship <u>won't</u> blast into space.

   A. can't

   B. will

   C. haven't

7. Jerry will fly <u>low</u> into space.

   A. over

   B. under

   C. high

8. Then, back to Earth he will <u>stop</u>.

   A. quit

   B. go

   C. end

Antonyms

Directions: Find a word in the box that means the opposite of each picture below. Print the word on the line.

happy	down	cold
go	day	finish
dry	nice	hate

1.

_____

2.

_____

3.

_____

4.

_____

5.

_____

6.

_____

7.

_____

8.

_____

9.

_____

Antonyms

Directions: Draw a line to match the words that mean the opposite. Write a story below using some of the **antonyms.**

1. wet		slow
2. up		shallow
3. opened		old
4. deep		dry
5. fast		closed
6. new		down

Homonyms

Directions: Find a word in the list below that sounds the same as each word. Print the **homonym** on the line.

meat	knead	blue	chews
Mrs.	one	buy	rows
eight	pain	scent	I

1. rose _____	**2.** cent _____	**3.** blew _____
4. won _____	**5.** meet _____	**6.** misses _____
7. by _____	**8.** choose _____	**9.** ate _____
10. eye _____	**11.** pane _____	**12.** need _____

Directions: Circle the correct **homonym** that will complete the sentence. Print it on the line.

13. She saw a _____ in the mountains.	dear deer
14. He played the _____ in the band.	symbols cymbals
15. Her mom _____ the beautiful dress.	sewed sowed
16. The boat was tied to the _____ .	dock doc

Homonyms

Directions: Print a word from the list below that sounds the same as each word, but is spelled differently and has a different meaning.

sent	rap	tale	not
pair	I	ours	flower
beau	nit	new	Sunday

1. sundae	**2.** flour	**3.** knot
_____	_____	_____
4. gnu	**5.** hours	**6.** tail
_____	_____	_____
7. knit	**8.** eye	**9.** wrap
_____	_____	_____
10. bow	**11.** pear	**12.** cent
_____	_____	_____

Homonyms

Directions: Print the correct **homonym** on the line to complete each sentence below.

	1. I saw the _____ building a hill.	aunts ants
	2. She wanted a slice of _____ .	bred bread
	3. Santa Claus has _____ reindeer.	ate eight
	4. The _____ was buzzing by the flower.	bee be
	5. The bunny loves to eat _____ .	carrots carets
	6. I saw the brown _____ at the zoo.	bare bear

Unit Review

Directions: Read the words in the box. Print the two words that belong under each heading.

Word List
disown
undo
ill
tail
return
tale
hot
distrust
unwind
rebuild
cold
sick

1. Two words that sound alike.

_____   _____

2. Two words that mean the same thing.

_____   _____

3. Two words that are opposite of each other.

_____   _____

4. Two words that begin with *re-*.

_____   _____

5. Two words that begin with *dis-*.

_____   _____

6. Two words that begin with *un-*.

_____   _____

Unit Review

Directions: Write a story about a trip to the zoo using at least five of the words in the box below.

Word List

bear

deer

unlocked

rewrite

disappeared

tail

awake

asleep

go

stop

tale

dear

night

day

_____

- -

_____

- -

_____

- -

_____

- -

_____

- -

_____

- -

_____

- -

_____

- -

_____

Unit Review

Directions: Fill in the bubble beside each word that names or describes each picture.

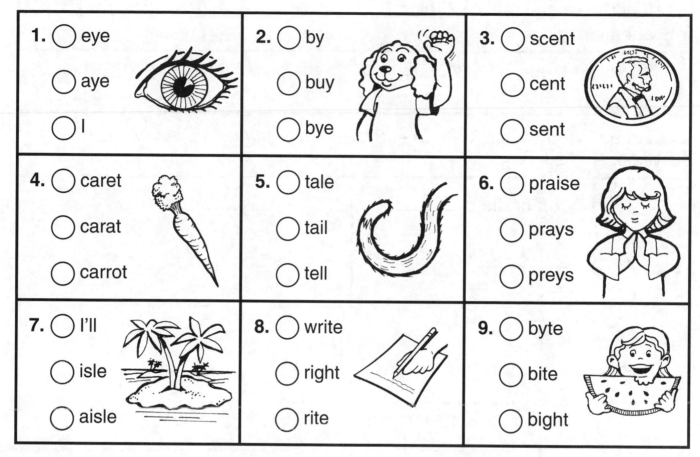

1. ◯ eye
   ◯ aye
   ◯ I

2. ◯ by
   ◯ buy
   ◯ bye

3. ◯ scent
   ◯ cent
   ◯ sent

4. ◯ caret
   ◯ carat
   ◯ carrot

5. ◯ tale
   ◯ tail
   ◯ tell

6. ◯ praise
   ◯ prays
   ◯ preys

7. ◯ I'll
   ◯ isle
   ◯ aisle

8. ◯ write
   ◯ right
   ◯ rite

9. ◯ byte
   ◯ bite
   ◯ bight

Directions: Fill in the bubble next to the word that means the opposite.

10. Opposite of sink ◯ float ◯ flat	**11.** Opposite of black ◯ white ◯ wait	**12.** Opposite of thin ◯ thick ◯ think
13. Opposite of stop ◯ go ◯ quit	**14.** Opposite of empty ◯ gone ◯ full	**15.** Opposite of shallow ◯ full ◯ deep
16. Opposite of few ◯ many ◯ money	**17.** Opposite of summer ◯ winter ◯ fall	**18.** Opposite of near ◯ far ◯ close

Unit Review

Directions: Circle the two words in each box that mean the same thing.

1. friend pal enemy girl	**2.** big small bag large	**3.** game gift present money
4. hope wish whale dish	**5.** happy glad sad said	**6.** little write right small

Directions: Add *un, dis,* or *re* to each base word to make a new word. Print the prefix on the line.

un or **dis**	**re** or **dis**
7. _____taste	**12.** _____pay
8. _____fair	**13.** _____trust
9. _____happy	**14.** _____do
10. _____appear	**15.** _____wind
11. _____pack	**16.** _____grace

Directions: Circle the word that will finish each sentence. Print the correct word on each line.

17. The _____ grew in the garden.	beats	beets
18. The sun rose in the _____ .	morning	evening
19. The giant _____ the troll.	disliked	unliked
20. The girl was very _____ .	unhappy	retry

Answer
Key

Answer Key

Page 5
1. Nn 9. Bb
2. Pp 10. Jj
3. Ll 11. Rr
4. Zz 12. Ss
5. Kk 13. Vv
6. Qq 14. Ff
7. Tt 15. Dd
8. Mm 16. Ff

Page 6
1. t 9. f
2. d 10. h
3. c 11. n
4. b 12. p
5. m 13. r
6. l 14. s
7. k 15. w
8. g 16. x

Page 7
1. k 9. c
2. f 10. l
3. r 11. q
4. x 12. s
5. b 13. t
6. d 14. g
7. m 15. w
8. p 16. h

Page 8
Below are sample answers.
1. hat 6. house
2. log 7. box
3. jig 8. ring
4. jeep 9. dock
5. boat 10. truck

Page 9
1. head 5. buzz
2. duck 6. bag
3. bat 7. pig
4. log 8. car

Page 10
1. p 9. s
2. l 10. m
3. t 11. r
4. d 12. k
5. b 13. l
6. f 14. n
7. g 15. t
8. x 16. n

Page 11
1. n 7. l 12. f
2. k 8. g 13. m
3. p 9. t 14. s
4. l 10. x 15. k
5. d 11. b 16. n
6. r

Page 12
1. b 7. t 12. s
2. z 8. x 13. m
3. m 9. k 14. t
4. p 10. d 15. r
5. p 11. w 16. s
6. n

Page 13
1. can 5. ran
2. bud 6. mat
3. pit 7. dot
4. sheet 8. kin

Page 14
1. bag 5. fan
2. hen 6. rug
3. cat 7. kid
4. fin 8. top

Page 15
1. p, g 9. g, m
2. d, g 10. s, n
3. c, t 11. d, r
4. b, r 12. r, t
5. w, b 13. t, n
6. h, t 14. m, p
7. r, g 15. l, p
8. b, g 16. r, n

Page 16
1. r, m 9. b, t
2. s, n 10. j, p
3. b, g 11. c, p
4. f, n 12. g, m
5. m, n 13. b, k
6. w, b 14. m, p
7. j, t 15. n, t
8. b, b 16. p, n

Page 17
1. v 9. d
2. l 10. s
3. g 11. m
4. t 12. t
5. g 13. d
6. x 14. t
7. v 15. b
8. m 16. x

Page 18
1. g 6. v
2. v 7. m
3. s 8. m
4. b 9. g
5. d 10. n

Page 19
1. g 9. g
2. t 10. t
3. l 11. l
4. t 12. n
5. r 13. t
6. m 14. l
7. m 15. b
8. p 16. d

Page 20
1. g 5. l
2. m 6. w
3. g 7. v
4. b 8. d

Page 21
1. sun 5. rat
2. rug 6. web
3. dog 7. can
4. fan 8. top

Page 22
1. log 5. bit
2. lot 6. bat
3. hot 7. cat
4. hit 8. rat

Page 23
1. bus 5. hit
2. hot 6. bat
3. fan 7. dog
4. can 8. cat

Page 24
1. bar 8. cat
2. bag 9. cut
3. tag 10. cot
4. tap 11. pot
5. top 12. hot
6. cop 13. hop
7. cap 14. top

Page 25
Stories will vary.

Page 26
1. pig 5. cow
2. bell 6. gum
3. hen 7. dress
4. dog 8. bed

Page 27
1. w 7. x
2. f 8. t
3. m 9. g
4. g 10. r
5. l 11. d
6. t 12. m

Page 29
1. cat 6. tap
2. van 7. band
3. dad 8. fan
4. sack 9. pan
5. ham 10. sad

Page 30
1. ram 7. yak
2. can 8. man
3. rat 9. hat
4. bat 10. ant
5. tag 11. cap
6. cat 12. ham

Page 31
Suggestions are listed.
cat—vat, bat, sat, mat
pan—tan, can, fan, man
sad—dad, mad, fad, lad
cab—jab, tab, gab, lab

Page 32
1. dig 6. kid
2. zip 7. mitt
3. sit 8. quill
4. fin 9. bin
5. sick 10. mill

Page 33
1. ribs 7. hill
2. fin 8. pig
3. wig 9. fish
4. bib 10. six
5. pill 11. lip
6. kid 12. pin

Page 34
1. wig 5. him
2. wish 6. fib
3. fix 7. rid
4. pip 8. tin

Page 35
1. cub 6. bug
2. club 7. sun
3. duck 8. hug
4. gum 9. rug
5. tub 10. run

Page 36
1. jug 8. drum
2. tub 9. gum
3. sun 10. sub
4. cut 11. cup or
5. hut mug
6. buzz 12. bus
7. bug

Page 37
sun—bun, pun, run, fun
jug—lug, pug, bug, mug
cup—hup, bup, pup, sup
sub—pub, rub, hub, tub

Page 38
1. hop 6. mop
2. sock 7. fox
3. pot 8. top
4. log 9. dog
5. box 10. rock

Page 39
1. log 7. fox
2. hop 8. cob
3. box 9. mop
4. doll 10. dog
5. pot 11. cot
6. top 12. ox

Page 40
job, cob cod, nod
mom, Tom toss, loss
rock, dock Don, Ron
fog, jog hop, top
cot, lot

Page 41
1. web 6. net
2. vest 7. eggs
3. deck 8. leg
4. pen 9. jet
5. hen 10. peck

Page 42
1. belt 7. bell
2. shell 8. men
3. net 9. bed
4. neck 10. nest
5. well 11. tent
6. desk 12. ten

Page 43

Page 44
short u—fuss, dug, bud
short a—ram, gap, rap
short e—yet, sell, led
short o—loss, pod, job
short i—hip, bid, pit

Page 45
1. hand 6. rock
2. fin 7. bat
3. bus 8. hen
4. doll 9. duck
5. bed

Page 46
1. The cat is on the sill.
2. The frog is on the lily pad.
3. The bug is in the net.
4. The pig is in the pen.
5. The dog ran in the sun.

Page 47
1. sis 5. beg
2. hop 6. bed
3. pup 7. log
4. Bob 8. fun

Page 48
1. jet 3. sun
2. sand 4. wet
5. Answers will vary.

Page 49
1. yes 7. no
2. no 8. yes
3. no 9. no
4. yes 10. no
5. no 11. yes
6. yes 12. yes

Page 50
1. u 7. u 12. i
2. i 8. e 13. u
3. a 9. e 14. e
4. e 10. o 15. o
5. a 11. a 16. i
6. o

Page 51
1. jet 7. mud
2. lock 8. kiss
3. bun 9. lap
4. pet 10. boss
5. big 11. bell
6. ax

Page 53
1. rake 7. plane
2. rain 8. wave
3. May 9. tape
4. tray 10. gate
5. cake 11. play
6. mail 12. game

Page 54
1. play 4. plane
2. Jane 5. day
3. games 6. rain

Page 55
1. lime 7. ride
2. ice 8. tide
3. mice 9. timer
4. tie 10. hike
5. pine 11. kite
6. dime 12. bike

Page 56
Short Vowel Sound—bit, sit, bid, rid, whip, six, sick
Long Vowel Sound—bite, ride, hide, side, slide, tide, wipe

Page 57
1. kite 6. bike
2. cake 7. mile
3. tail 8. paint
4. dime 9. time
5. rain

Page 58
1. rose 7. joker
2. road 8. bone
3. soap 9. nose
4. boat 10. hose
5. goat 11. rope
6. coat 12. notes

Page 59
1. owned 4. bowl
2. Joe 5. hole
3. bone 6. nose

Page 60
1. music 7. cube
2. ruler 8. suit
3. fruit 9. flute
4. bugle 10. tube
5. glue 11. clue
6. June 12. mule

Page 61
1. flute 6. music
2. tune 7. use
3. lute 8. glue
4. bugle 9. blue
5. tuba 10. flu

Page 62
1. soap 6. flute
2. tube 7. cubes
3. drove 8. blue
4. note 9. music
5. rope 10. wrote

Page 63
1. jeans 7. tree
2. bead 8. pea
3. three 9. jeep
4. beet 10. seal
5. bee 11. eat
6. seat 12. feet

Page 64
Stories will vary.

Page 65
Long e—feet, street, free, east, Easter, seen, bead, meal
Long i—side, dime, kite, nine, bike, bile, pine, bite, pie, mile, site, hike
Long o—coat, boat, choke, broke, goat, mole, cope, rope

Page 66
Stories will vary.

Page 67
1. o, short
2. o, short
3. a, long
4. i, long
5. e, long
6. e, short
7. a, short
8. u, long
9. o, long
10. i, short
11. i, long
12. i, long
13. e, long
14. u, short
15. e, long
16. e, long
17. u, long
18. a, long
19. o, long
20. o, short

Page 68
1. long 12. short
2. long 13. long
3. long 14. long
4. short 15. short
5. long 16. long
6. long 17. short
7. long 18. short
8. short 19. short
9. short 20. long
10. long 21. long
11. long

Page 69
1. rat, bat
2. went, dent
3. bun, fun
4. gate, bate
5. like, hike
6. boat, coat
7. nap, sap
8. bit, hit
9. hot, cot
10. heat, beat
11. hut, but
12. bake, cake
13. sea, tea
14. bud, dud
15. kite, site
16. wig, fig
17. nose, hose
18. hop, cop
19. fog, log
20. wave, save

Answer Key

Page 70
Answers may vary.
1. bite   13. can
2. pane   14. pan
3. said   15. ran
4. read   16. kit
5. rain   17. wed
6. weed   18. hop
7. tone   19. fin
8. bait   20. rob
9. hope   21. set
10. cone   22. bat
11. rate   23. cub
12. fate   24. tub

Page 71
Long Vowel Sound—
kite, nine, bike, goat, coat, feet, tail, bean, tube, cube, goes
Short Vowel Sound—
sock, hat, net, doll, duck, fish, tack, bed, bag, cub

Page 72
Long a—tape, bay, nail
Long e—feet, bean, seed
Long i—white, time, line
Long o—goat, vote, bow
Long u—fuse, tube, mule

Page 73

r	i	e	f	l	o	a	t
b	a	k	e	a	w	p	a
i	e	a	e	a	r	l	c
w	a	i	t	a	i	a	u
a	p	b	o	a	t	t	t
j	e	a	n	s	e	o	e
s	u	i	t	t	o	i	e
a	k	i	t	e	p	e	a

Stories will vary.

Page 74
1. cake   6. gate
2. cute   7. boat
3. blue   8. kite
4. bike   9. feet
5. beans   10. coat

Page 75
Long a—ray, rain, train, tape, mail, take, nail
Long e—jeans, feel, lead, seat, teen
Long i—time, nine, bike, pie, ride
Long o—bow, hole, note, boat, hope
Long u—use, mule, tube, fuse, lute, flute

Page 77
1. doghouse
2. snowman
3. seashell
4. bluebird
5. beehive
6. doorbell
7. bedroom
8. teapot

Page 78
1. 1   8. 2
2. 2   9. 2
3. 2   10. 1
4. 1   11. 1
5. 2   12. 1
6. 1   13. 2
7. 1   14. 2

Page 79
hill (1)
popcorn (2)
eagle (2)
games (1)
car (1)
cabin (2)
candles (2)
backpack (2)
1. cabin
2. backpack
3. hill
4. games
5. eagle
6. candles
7. popcorn
8. car

Page 80
1. rattle
2. candle
3. bubble
4. saddle
5. bottle
6. cattle
7. middle
8. noodles
9. beagle
10. ladle
11. castle
12. handle

Page 81
1. soft   8. hard
2. hard   9. soft
3. hard   10. hard
4. soft   11. hard
5. soft   12. hard
6. hard   13. soft
7. soft   14. soft

Page 82
1. hard   8. hard
2. soft   9. hard
3. soft   10. soft
4. hard   11. hard
5. hard   12. soft
6. soft   13. soft
7. soft   14. hard

Page 83
Hard c—cuff, cone, cast, cob, cane, cut
Soft c—cyst, cent, city, nice, citrus, recess
Hard g—gust, go, gull, gap, gobble, gallon
Soft g—gym, sage, giant, judge, barge, ginger

Page 84
1. fl   8. sp
2. sn   9. dr
3. fr   10. pl
4. sl   11. st
5. br   12. cr
6. pr   13. cl
7. tr   14. gl

Page 85
plum, stairs, crib
prince, blocks, swings
bridge, snow, glass
1. stairs   5. glass
2. snow   6. prince
3. plum   7. bridge
4. crib   8. swings
        9. blocks

Page 86
1. golf   8. sand
2. pants   9. west
3. gift   10. sling
4. lamp   11. melt
5. toast   12. film
6. milk   13. raft
7. bank   14. gymnast

Page 87
1. squirrel   7. swings
2. snakes   8. smile
3. bank   9. blue
4. bride   10. class
5. grass   11. dress
6. trap   12. drum

Page 88
1. sleepy   6. sly
2. funny   7. why
3. happy   8. try
4. tiny   9. by
5. hurry   10. my

Page 89
1. mommy—fuzzy why—thy
2. frilly—dizzy ply—try
3. Ky—sky daddy—marry
4. by—pry dairy—Sally
5. long e
6. long i
7. long i
8. long e
9. long i
10. long e
11. long i
12. long e

Page 90
1. thumbs, yes
2. Shells, no
3. cherry, yes
4. think, yes
5. Shoes, yes
6. duck, no
7. chair, yes
8. whistle, no
9. wick, yes
10. shuttle, yes
11. whale, yes
12. teeth, no
13. ship, yes

Page 91
1. knee   6. knob
2. knit   7. knock
3. knight   8. knew
4. knife   9. kneel
5. know

Page 92
1. wrench   7. wrap
2. wreath   8. wrist
3. wreck   9. write
4. wren   10. wriggle
5. wrong   11. wrinkle
6. wrestle

Page 93
1. sh   9. ch
2. wr, ch   10. kn
3. ch   11. ch
4. th   12. wh
5. sh   13. wh
6. th   14. ck
7. wh   15. wr
8. kn   16. th

Page 94
1. car   6. arms
2. start   7. dark
3. farm   8. jar
4. barn   9. star
5. hard

Page 95
Column 1: 1, 3, 1, 3, 1
Column 2: 3, 2, 2, 1, 2

Page 96
1. circus
2. nurse
3. river
4. turkey
5. purse
6. hammer
7. shirt
8. computer
9. letters
10. girl
11. turtle
12. bird

Page 97
ar—dart, card, far, bark
or—form, storm, store, torch, sort
ir—sir, first, dirt, chirp, fir
er—her, verse, over, perk, serve
ur—purr, burst, burn, turn, fur

Page 98
1. gobble
2. sunny
3. drum
4. clock
5. garbage
6. shy
7. birdcage
8. thimble
9. ice
10. flashlight
11. porch
12. wrist
13. twins
14. brush
15. farm
16. batter

Page 99
1. shy
2. Sally
3. castle
4. letter
5. mailbox
6. giant
7. white
8. lunch
9. table
10. fork
11. ice cream
12. dragon

Page 101
1. Do not
2. It is
3. We have
4. have not
5. will not
6. aren't
7. didn't
8. he's
9. that's
10. we've
11. don't
12. won't
13. she's
14. I've
15. they've

Page 102
1. I am
2. We are
3. Let us
4. I will
5. He will
6. we'll
7. I'm
8. we're
9. let's
10. they'll
11. he'll
12. you're
13. I'll
14. they're
15. she'll

Page 103
1. We'll
2. doesn't
3. He'll
4. it's
5. We've
6. I'm
7. won't
8. She'll
9. we're
10. I'm
11. They'll
12. It's

Page 104
1. It's   6. he'll
2. Who's   7. she'll
3. I'm   8. They'd
4. I'll   9. Let's
5. we'll   10. We're

Page 105
1. animals
2. elephants
3. foxes
4. hippopotamuses
5. peaches

Page 106
1. s   6. es
2. es   7. es
3. s   8. es
4. s   9. s
5. es   10. es

Page 107
1. walked
2. raining
3. climbing
4. played
5. jumping
6. being
7. starting
8. sleeping

Page 108
1. swimming
2. shopping
3. rubbing
4. grinning
5. stopping
6. trotting
7. running
8. hopping

Page 109
1. pinned
2. robbed
3. stopped
4. planned
5. tapped
6. grinned
7. shipped
8. rubbed

Page 110
1. voted
2. baking
3. sliced
4. firing
5. diced
6. saving, saved
7. icing, iced

Page 111
1. pinning
2. saving
3. cleaning
4. skipping
5. waving
6. walking
7. stomping
8. poking
9. swinging
10. riding
11. hopping
12. hoping
13. skipped
14. walked
15. skated
16. played
17. pinned

Page 112
Stories will vary.

Page 113
1. playful   9. slow
2. helpful   10. cheer
3. hopeful   11. care
4. quickly   12. use
5. hopeful   13. wish
6. playful   14. loud
7. helpful   15. quick
8. quickly   16. brave

Page 114
1. goodness
2. darkness
3. homeless
4. moonless
5. moonless
6. darkness
7. homeless
8. goodness

Page 115
1. quietly
2. happiness
3. softness
4. sleepless
5. joyful
6.–10. Sentences will vary.

Page 116
1. softer, softest
2. greater, greatest
3. faster, fastest
4. shorter, shortest
5. cuter, cutest
6. stranger, strangest
7. harder, hardest
8. smaller, smallest
9. madder, maddest
10. smarter, smartest

Page 117
1. rainiest or rainier
2. chillier
3. sunniest
4. windiest or windier
5. fluffiest
6. snowiest

Answer Key

Page 118
1. bunnies
2. cherries
3. daisies
4. cities
5. parties
6. pennies
7. candies
8. ponies
9. lilies
10. puppies
11. stories
12. families
13. strawberries
14. babies
15. dairies

Page 119
ed—rested, jumped
ing—coming, making
ly—quickly, lowly
ful—helpful, careful
es—patches, brushes
ness—darkness,
happiness
er—cloudier, smarter
est—silliest
contractions—Answers
will vary.

Page 120
1. ed
2. es
3. ing
4. ful
5. est
6. ly, es
7. er
8. ly, n't
9. est

Page 121
Stories will vary.

Page 122
1. fox
2. baker
3. dishes
4. reading
5. teacher
6. cherries
7. peaches
8. singing
9. taller
10. playing
11. rubbing
12. running

Page 123
1. softly
2. watched
3. sledding
4. hardly
5. darkness
6. happily
7. jumped
8. scariest
9. swished
10. couldn't

Page 125
1. sail
2. brain
3. mail
4. pay
5. pail
6. pray
7. May
8. train
9. ray
10. hail

Page 126
1. tree
2. teach
3. knee
4. wreath
5. steam
6. beads
7. beach
8. meat
9. tea
10. peach

Page 127
1. The cat will lie down.
2. Water your plant or it will die.
3. Her hoe is broken.
4. My brother is named Joe.
5. We made an apple pie.

Page 128
1. moat
2. coat
3. rowboat
4. crow
5. bowl
6. mow
7. blow
8. float

Page 129

sun
bay
dig
cat
bite
say
keep
top
got
deal
leaf
bee
clay
tie
rail
lie
toe
bug
pie
tin
goat
bowl
boat

Page 130
1. tail
2. hay
3. drain
4. bleed
5. dream
6. green
7. feel
8. neat
9. toes
10. doe
11. boat
12. rainbow
13. slow

Page 131
1. moon
2. pool
3. broom
4. moose
5. tooth
6. goose
7. varoom
8. boom
9. boo
10. moo
11. coo
12. goo
13. too
14. Achoo

Page 132
1. book
2. hood
3. brook
4. cook
5. wood
6. hook
7. good
8. wood
9. hood
10. hook
11. took
12. look
13. nook
14. rook

Page 133
Column 1: 1, 2, 3, 3, 2
Column 2: 3, 1, 2, 1, 3

Page 134

		P						
	h	a	u	l				
		u			s	a	w	
		l						
			c	r	a	w	l	
							a	
				r			w	
				a			s	
	d			w				
	r							
	a							
	w							
l	a	w	n					

Page 135
1. fawn
2. bread
3. cookie
4. good
5. hawk
6. cool
7. pause
8. ready
9. brook
10. loose
11. bawl
12. groom
13. Heather

Page 136
Check to make sure directions are followed correctly.

Page 137
Check to make sure all words are matched to their pictures.

Page 138
Correct path: wow, now, scowl, crowd, cowboy, growl, prowl, howl, drown, town, frown, down, clown, flower, how, fowl, brown, shower, owl, towel, power, brow, cow, pow, crown, gown, chow

Page 139
house, flowers
1. town
2. plow
3. ground
4. trowel
5. mound
6. cloud
7. brow
8. showers
crowds, proud

Page 140
1. c
2. d
3. a
4. b
5. h
6. g
7. f
8. e
9. j
10. k
11. l
12. i

Page 141
oi—coil, poise, joint
oy—coy, Floyd, soy
oi—choice, poise, foil

Page 142
1. Roy
2. Joy
3. boys
4. toys
5. spoiled
6. soy
7. coins
8. broil
9. choice
10. boil
11. foil
12. noise
13. Joyce
14. oil
15. enjoy

Page 143
1. mew, no
2. new, yes
3. screw, no
4. stew, yes
5. chew, yes
6. news, no
7. blew, yes
8. Few, no
9. grew, no
10. flew, yes
11. threw, yes
12. knew, yes
13. flew, no

Page 144
1. clown
2. toys
3. stew
4. soil
5. house
6. screw
7. mew
8. coins
9. boy
10. cloud
11. flew
12. crown

Page 145
1. town
2. beach
3. see
4. tail
5. feather
6. bowl
7. die
8. boys
9. moat
10. foes
11. zoo
12. yawn
13. train
14. day
15. took
16. mew

Page 146
1. oo
2. ai
3. aw
4. ie
5. oa
6. oo
7. ee
8. ie
9. ou
10. ow
11. oo
12. ew
13. oo
14. ea
15. aw
16. oy

Page 147
1. brain
2. peep
3. toes
4. food
5. cook
6. wood
7. breakfast
8. growl
9. noon
10. yawn
11. jaw
12. point
13. crew
14. bowl
15. Joy

Page 148
1. coins
2. grew
3. beach
4. zoo
5. house
6. soap
7. breath
8. pause
9. found
10. tie
11. boy
12. mow
13. gray

Page 150
1. rebuild
2. redo
3. refilled
4. replay
5. remake
6. replaced
7. refuel
8. recheck

Page 151
1. build
2. wrap
3. name
4. direct
5. play
6. use
7. view
8. make
9. write
10. check

Page 152
1. unequal
2. unlikely
3. unforseen
4. unnecessary
5. unpopular
6. undress
7. unlawful
8. unusual
9. unseen
10. undo

Page 153
unhappy, undressed
unbuttoned, undone
unlocked, untied
unbuckled, unpacked
Stories will vary.

Page 154

r	e	c	l	a	i	m	t	y	u
e	u	n	c	o	v	e	r	i	n
g	n	r	o	r	e	u	s	e	u
a	s	e	p	a	u	n	f	i	t
i	a	z	r	x	d	u	u	m	i
n	f	e	r	e	d	o	l	j	e
c	e	a	v	w	b	n	l	o	m
s	d	y	f	r	g	h	o	a	j
k	r	e	p	a	c	k	c	a	l
r	e	r	e	p	r	e	k	d	r

Page 155
1. rewrite
2. uncomfortable
3. retell
4. review
5. unhappy
6. unfair
7. repack
8. return

Page 156
1. disappear
2. dislike
3. disgrace
4. disclose
5. disloyal
6. disobey
7. disagree
8. discover
9. distrust
10. distaste

Page 157
1. disagree
2. disbelieve
3. discolor
4. disconnected
5. distaste
6. dishonest
7. disjoin
8. disobey
9. distrust

Page 158
1. uneasy
2. unable
3. unhappy
4. dislike
5. reminded

Page 159
un—unhappy, undress, unbutton, unkind, unlucky, untie
dis—disagree, disapprove, disobey, distrust, disloyal, displease, discolor
re—remove, regain, rebrush, rewind, reorder, redo, remove

Page 160
1. huge
2. sick
3. garbage
4. friend
5. giggle
6. small
Suggestions are listed below.
7. thin
8. bad
9. comfortable
10. sleep
11. like
12. talk
13. hate
14. happy

Page 161
Across
1. lie
2. man
8. pony
9. quick
Down
3. buy
4. hope
5. small
6. dirt
7. huge

Page 162
1. pal—friend
2. laugh—giggle
3. kind—nice
4. glad—happy
5. grin—smile
6. celebration—party
Stories will vary.

Page 163
1. B
2. C
3. A
4. B
5. C
6. B
7. C
8. B

Page 164
1. down
2. dry
3. go
4. happy
5. cold
6. nice
7. finish
8. hate
9. day

Page 165
1. wet—dry
2. up—down
3. opened—closed
4. deep—shallow
5. fast—slow
6. new—old
Stories will vary.

Page 166
1. rows
2. scent
3. blue
4. one
5. meat
6. Mrs.
7. buy
8. chews
9. eight
10. I
11. pain
12. knead
13. deer
14. cymbals
15. sewed
16. dock

Page 167
1. Sunday
2. flower
3. not
4. new
5. ours
6. tale
7. nit
8. I
9. rap
10. beau
11. pair
12. sent

Page 168
1. ants
2. bread
3. eight
4. bee
5. carrots
6. bear

Page 169
1. tail, tale
2. ill, sick
3. cold, hot
4. rebuild, return
5. distrust, disown
6. unwind, undo

Page 170
Stories will vary.

Page 171
1. eye
2. bye
3. cent
4. carrot
5. tail
6. prays
7. isle
8. write
9. bite
10. float
11. white
12. thick
13. go
14. full
15. deep
16. many
17. winter
18. far

Page 172
1. friend, pal
2. big, large
3. present, gift
4. hope, wish
5. happy, glad
6. little, small
7. dis
8. un
9. un
10. dis
11. un
12. re
13. dis
14. re
15. re
16. dis
17. beets
18. morning
19. disliked
20. unhappy